THE
CREATIVE
KID'S
GUIDE
TO
HOME
COMPUTERS

FRED D'IGNAZIO

THE CREATIVE KID'S GUIDE TO HOME COMPUTERS

Super Games and Projects
To Do with Your Home Computer

Doubleday & Company, Inc., Garden City, New York

Interior of book designed by Virginia M. Soulé
Line drawings by Stan Gilliam

Library of Congress Cataloging in Publication Data

D'Ignazio, Fred.
  The creative kid's guide to home computers.

  Bibliography: p. 102
  Includes index.
  SUMMARY: Explains what home computers do and suggests
ways to use them for games and projects.
  1. Microcomputers—Juvenile literature.
2. Minicomputers—Juvenile literature. 3. Electronic
data processing—Juvenile literature.
[1. Microcomputers. 2. Minicomputers. 3. Electronic
data processing. 4. Computers] I. Title.
QA76.5.D4963   001.64
Library of Congress Catalog Card Number 79–6860
ISBN: 0-385-15313-9 Trade
ISBN: 0-385-15314-7 Library

FOR
ERIC
Alias
"The Commando Kid"

I am indebted to all those who helped make this book possible. I am particularly grateful to the following:

To *Omni* Magazine for permission to reprint from Dr. Christopher Evans's interview with chessmaster David Levy (OMNI, April 1979, page 64–67 and 133–34).

To Alan Kay, Adele Goldberg, and the Xerox PARC scientists and educators for their insights into using small computers to build models of our world.

To Nancy Connors for her expert suggestions and advice concerning my chapter on "Helping a Friend."

To Ray Puechner for the idea for this book, and for putting me in touch with my publisher.

To Roy Wandelmaier for his patience, his support, and his careful editing.

To Janet Letts D'Ignazio for helping me prepare the Glossary and Index; and for putting up with me during the many months it took to write this book.

CONTENTS

THE
CREATIVE
KID'S
GUIDE
TO
HOME
COMPUTERS

INTRODUCTION

THE "WHAT IF . . .?" MACHINES

The day your family gets a home computer will be a thrill. But it won't be long—days, maybe hours—before you'll start to grow bored with the first few things the computer can do. You'll want to make its games more challenging and exciting; its chores more useful and practical. You'll want to experiment with the computer and plug it into things: the TV, the stereo, even the smoke alarm. You'll want the computer to make pictures that are colorful and full of action. You'll want it to make music. You'll want it to talk and listen.

"What if . . . ?" you'll wonder. "What if I did math homework on the computer? What if I used it to write book reports and research papers? What if I composed my own music on the computer? What if I used it to play science games, strategy games, sports games, and fantasy games? What if I invented totally new games?

"Or what if I locked the family computer with secret codes that no outsider could crack? What if I taught it to write poetry? What if I used it to draw pictures—moving pictures of horses, cartoons, or spinning planets? What if I used it to plot my biorhythm or horoscope?

"Or what if I used the computer to help a friend of mine who's deaf? What if I turned the computer into a baby-sitter—and a teacher—for my little sister? What if I plugged it into a robot?

"Or what if I used the computer to set up a foolproof burglar alarm? What if I tied it into the telephone or cable TV and used it to send "electronic mail" to my friends? What if I fed it emergency information like antidotes to poisons? Or what if . . . ?"

COMPUTERS FOR EVERYONE

What makes a home computer so special? It is special because it is a new medium of human communication. It is radically different from all other media, yet its development is similar to that of the book—only in forty years rather than five hundred. Like the big early computers, books were originally the property of only a few individuals and institutions rich enough to afford them. With the development of the printing press, and later the Industrial Revolution, books could be mass-produced, and they became inexpensive. Everyone could buy them. Similarly, with the birth of the new space-age technology that has shrunk computers from warehouse-sized monsters to chips even smaller than your fingernail, computers are becoming easy to afford, too. Like books, they will soon appear in everyone's home.

Who will benefit the most from the new home computers? You will. Many older people still see computers as giant brains with plans to take over the world. Since they fear computers and distrust them, they are unprepared to learn how they work, and take advantage of their marvelous talents. You, on the other hand, will work with computers in your own home, get to know them up close, and have the chance to learn what makes them work. You'll find that a home computer is what you make it. You can play games with it, train it like a pet, or use it to teach you and exercise your mind.

A home computer is also a great listener. This is what separates it from a TV or radio, you can watch, listen to, and enjoy them, but you can't talk back.* The computer is different: You have to give it commands to make it work; you have to answer its questions, and guide and direct everything it does. You can't sit passively in front of it. Whether you're playing it in a game or feeding it new commands, you have to look sharp and put your mind in gear. Don't ever let it catch you napping.

BUILDING MODELS

Have you ever built a model car or airplane? You can use a computer to build models—not out of plastic, wood, or glue, but using a picture screen and a light-pen or the keys on a typewriter. A home computer's most outstanding feature is that it gives you the ability to *simulate*, to create models of the real world. In the near future, you could learn how to build computer models as naturally as you now write words on a page. You might build beautiful, artistic models of sight and sound; ele-

---

* Using a hand-held control box, you will be able to talk back to two-way cable and "Teletext" TVs. But whom will you be talking to? A computer, of course.

gant, scientific models of our universe; or game models of realistic or fantastic adventure.

Home computers will soon be simple enough for everyone to operate —in low gear. If you want to learn how to use all of the wonderful features a home computer can offer, you'll need to learn more about them. You can start with this book. It introduces you to home computers, then gives you a look at some games you can play, projects and experiments you can try, and models you can build. It finishes with a chapter on home computers of the future, and a set of appendices and a glossary to help you get started.

Just remember, this book is not a cookbook, it's an idea book. It won't teach you how to program or how to build your own computer. There already are dozens of excellent books that teach you how to do that. (Just take a look at Appendix A.)

Brandon Rigney of Arlington, Texas, built a computer model of the energy it takes to create a certain lighting pattern in a room. Architects can use Brandon's model to help them decide on the most energy-saving arrangement of light fixtures in a new building. Brandon built the model on his home computer, a *TRS-80* made by Radio Shack.

This book doesn't explain to you "how to," it encourages you to ask "What if . . . ?" It should tickle your curiosity and unleash your imagination. It should make you uncomfortable with what home computers can do today, and make you wonder about the things you might make them do tomorrow. Take a look at the games and projects in this book. How many more can you dream up on your own?

A WHIRLWIND
TOUR

IT CAN SOLVE A PROBLEM

What does a home computer do? *It reshapes information.* For example, it can accept questions and give back answers. This makes it a problem-solver. But to solve problems, the computer needs information. The information, known as *data*, is stored in the computer's *memory*. The memory looks like a window screen under a magnifying glass, with hundreds of tiny, crisscrossing wires. At each point where the wires cross, there's a memory *storage cell*, like a pigeonhole or mailbox, which holds a *datum* (a single piece of data). Grouped together, these data might be satellite reports on world weather patterns, rules of French grammar, the parts of a nuclear reactor, the activity of cancerous lung cells, or your math homework.

The computer cannot invent a solution to a problem. It isn't magic; it's just very, very fast. For a computer to solve a problem, you need to give it specific steps to follow. How do you give it these steps? First, you sit down and figure them out. Then you translate each step into orders—or *commands*—to the computer, using a special English-like computer *language*. All the commands together—all the steps needed to solve your problem—are known as a *program*.

IT'S A MACHINE . . .

A home computer is a *machine*. Inside the machine are its parts—its wires, buttons, and lights. These parts are known as its *hardware*. A home computer runs on electricity. It regulates electrical pressure, or *voltage*, to

Today's home computers fit on a desk and consume the power of a light bulb, yet are faster, have more memory, and are more powerful than the warehouse-sized computers of the early 1950s. Pictured here is one of the first "wizard computers": the *Apple II* made by Apple Computer, Inc. [Courtesy of Apple Computer, Inc.]

be either on or off, high or low. Voltage pulses whisk across the computer's tiny wires at intervals of less than a millionth of a second. Each pulse represents a single unit, or *bit*, of information. When the voltage is on, or high, it carries a "1" bit. When it is off, or low, it carries a "0." These bits represent the computer's *binary*, or *digital, machine language*. Grouped together, they form the *commands* (the "programs") and the *information* (the "data") that the computer processes. When eight voltages—eight "1's" and "0's"—get together, they form a *byte*. Depending on the situation a byte can be a command (like RUN this game), a character, or letter (like the letter A), or a *binary* number (a "00000101" in *binary* is a "5" in decimal). The computer uses *binary* numbers when it does arithmetic. All of the computer's voltages—its bits and bytes—are stored, a bit at a time, in memory; or shot across wires, a bit at a time, to be processed by the computer's electronic brain.*

* See Appendix E for tables of bits and bytes.

. . . A MACHINE THAT FOLLOWS A PLAN

A computer's program, or *software*, is made up of thousands of individual bits and bytes. It is the *plan* that controls the machine. It might be the rules of your favorite game, directions on what to do if the computer sees a burglar, instructions on how to decipher secret messages, or a method to translate musical notes into sound. There are three kinds of plans—or *programs*: ones that are stored permanently inside the computer's memory (like in a digital watch); ones that are stored in a memory cartridge that can be plugged into the computer (like on video games); and ones that you make up yourself and store in the computer's memory temporarily.

The type of program you make up yourself is called a *user* or *application program*. You write this type of program to make the computer do something useful—solve a problem, play a game, or help you study for a test. The other two types of programs, which come with the machine, or which you buy separately, are called *control* or *system programs*. One control program you can't do without is known as a *monitor* or *operating system*. It is usually stored on the computer at the factory. It oversees and co-ordinates all the different parts of the computer and keeps them working together.

Interpreters are another kind of control program. An interpreter is a lot like a monitor. Interpreters and monitors let you give commands to different parts of the computer—commands for storing information, printing it out, erasing it, and saving it. An interpreter, however, also lets you write, store, and run your own programs. It recognizes twenty or thirty different English-like commands. Grouped together, the commands form a program. Depending on which commands you use, the program might add two numbers, list all the stereo albums you own, draw pictures, or make music.

There is another kind of program called a *compiler*. Compiler and interpreter programs translate your commands into the electric signals that guide and direct the computer. There are many kinds of compilers and interpreters on home computers. One of the most widely used interpreters is called BASIC (*Beginner's All-purpose Symbolic Instruction Code*). It will be used for all the examples in this book.

SMALLER THAN YOUR THUMBNAIL

What sets a home computer apart from all the giant computers of the past is the tiny *chip*—a maze of miniature wires on a ¼-inch square of silicon. There are three main parts to a home computer: two kinds of memory, and a unit that obeys the commands given to the computer. A home computer is so small because each of these main parts fits on a chip.

First, there is the *ROM* (*Read Only Memory*) chip. When you buy a home computer, a ROM chip is often inside with one or more programs stored on it while the computer was still at the factory. These programs would certainly include a monitor, and, possibly, also an interpreter or compiler. Once stored on ROM, the programs cannot be erased, even when the computer is turned off.

Manufacturers also store special music, color, and game programs on ROM chips. They place the chips inside *cartridges*, or *game packs*, which can be plugged into many video (TV) games and home computers.

There is another kind of memory chip known as *RAM* (*Random Access Memory*). RAM is the computer's main memory. Unlike ROM, it is erased each time you turn off the computer. When you turn the computer back on, all the little memory cells in RAM are empty. It's up to

Home computers are so small because their memory and their processing unit (or brain) each fit on a *chip*—a maze of tiny wires crisscrossing a thin square of silicon only one-quarter inch on a side. Pictured below is the *Intel 8748 CPU* (Central Processing Unit) chip, complete with a clock and some scratchpad memory. [Courtesy Intel Corporation.]

you, with the help of the monitor program, to fill RAM—with programs and data.

The third type of chip is the *CPU* (*Central Processing Unit*). The CPU is where information is reshaped, where commands are obeyed. The CPU receives data and commands from both of the computer's memories —RAM and ROM—but it can store only new data or commands on RAM. While only one command at a time can come through the CPU, it is still capable of obeying—or *executing*—up to 70,000 commands a second! Also, the CPU is familiar with up to 250 different elementary commands. These enable it to make decisions, do arithmetic, and juggle letters and words.

HOW TO USE IT

The way to get information into a home computer is by pushing a button—on a typewriter keyboard or a game control panel. The way to get information out is just as simple: The computer types it out on a small, calculatorlike display of *LEDs* (*Light Emitting Diodes*), on a picture screen, or on a piece of paper in the computer typewriter or terminal.

With the proper attachments, or *add-ons*, you don't have to type a message to the computer—you can talk to it. Likewise, the computer doesn't have to print its answer—it can flash lights, buzz, ring bells, play music, or even talk.

The RAM, ROM, and CPU chips are all plugged into plastic *PC* (*printed circuit*) *boards*, or *cards*, inside a metal box known as the *mainframe*. Before you run a program (through the computer's "brain"— its CPU), you must store it in RAM, the computer's main memory. What happens to the data and commands stored in RAM when you turn off the computer? They're erased. If you have a game program stored in RAM, and you're ready to turn off the computer, of course you don't want to lose it, so you need another form of memory for your home computer: *removable* or *mass memory*. There are two main types of removable memory: tape cassettes and floppy disks. They are not as fast as RAM, but they are capable of storing much greater quantities of programs and data.

Almost everyone is familiar with *tape cassettes*. They fit into a standard, low-cost audio cassette recorder. Once the recorder is plugged into the computer, you can use the control program—either a monitor or interpreter—to send a copy of your program from RAM to the tape cassette. This is possible with the use of a converter that translates the computer's electronic signals to audio *tones* (sounds), which can be stored on the tape cassette.

A *floppy disk* looks like a record in a protective case. A record

Home computers have many attachments that make them more powerful and easy to use. Pictured above is the *Atari 800*, one of the first "wizard" computers. The computer's brain (CPU) and its onboard memory (RAM and ROM) are all hidden inside the typewriter case. Attachments for the computer include a picture screen (center), a tape recorder (left), and dual disk drives (right) for storage of programs and data when the computer is turned off. [Courtesy of Atari, Inc.]

"stores" music; the floppy disk stores information. A floppy disk fits into a *floppy-disk drive*. Once the drive is plugged into the computer, you can use the control program to send a copy of your program from RAM to the floppy disk.

Floppy-disk drives are more expensive than tape recorders, but the price of floppy-disk drives is dropping dramatically, and they are more reliable, faster, and easier to use.

EVERYWHERE BUT THE KITCHEN SINK

Before you know it, there will be dozens of computers in your home. In fact, it is impossible to list all the home computers that will soon appear. Since there is no limit to people's imagination, the list would be infinite: It would never end.

One thing we do know: Most of the computers already entering the home are *special-purpose*, or *nonprogrammable, computers*. Like the electric motor, special-purpose computers will soon be hidden in virtually all household appliances—washing machines, ovens, bathroom scales, typewriters, telephones—you name it.

Where else can you find computers in the home? Inside calculators, hand-held and video games, children's toys, and, recently, inside robots.

Last, but not least, come the *general-purpose computers*—the computers you can program yourself. There are dozens of brand names to choose from, but only a few types: the hobbyist kits, the inexpensive computers, the business and professional computers, and the game-and-learning computers (I call them the "wizards"). Wizards are the latest—and most exciting—type of home computer. You can program them yourself, or you can pop in a canned program on a cartridge or cassette. Wizards talk, accept voice commands, make noises, play music, and draw colorful pictures. They can teach you Spanish, plot your biorhythm, and play a mean game of *Hangman*.

GAMES

BEAT
THE
COMPUTER!

In a single afternoon, where can you bet at a noisy racetrack, have a shootout in the Old West, score a goal in a crowded soccer stadium, and battle a fleet of alien space cruisers millions of light-years from earth? In your living room, playing home-computer games—complete with color, sound effects, and plenty of action!

A game is really a *model*, or *simulation*, of some real or imagined situation. For example, a crimefighter game simulates the way a detective or a policeman battles crime in the real world. The game is exciting because it reminds you of the adventure, the suspense, and the danger faced by a real crimefighter. It is also exciting because you play the part of the crimefighter. You feel his emotions. You make his decisions. A *computer* game is especially exciting because it creates the illusion of reality; because, as a model, it closely resembles the real world. It moves fast, it makes decisions, it keeps you on your toes, and it has sound effects and animated pictures. As the computer becomes more sophisticated, the game becomes more convincing, more real.

SPORTS GAMES

There are dozens of hand-held computer sports games. Take Coleco's *Electronic Football*. You can choose to play the computer or play a friend. On the offense, you can run, kick, block, and pass. On the defense, you can intercept passes, tackle, and even blitz the quarterback. The *LED* display gives you your *stats*: time, score, downs, yards to go, and field position.

Mattel's hand-held football game is similar to Coleco's. With Mat-

A hand-held game like Mattel's *Baseball* is really a tiny special-purpose computer that is programmed to do only one thing: play ball! [Courtesy of Mattel, Inc.]

tel's *Football II* you can also punt, kick field goals, and reverse your field. Both games have two levels of playing difficulty. Sound effects include a ref's whistle, a cheer or victory tune after each score, and a charge on kickoff.

There are many other hand-held sports games, including basketball, hockey, soccer, and auto racing. Mattel's *Electronic Baseball* is particularly exciting. Your team is up to bat, and the computer's team is on the field. You control hitting and base running. The computer pitcher is tough: It throws fast balls, curves, and change-ups. There are game sounds for hits, outs, home runs, and a special sound effect at the end of each game.

OUTWIT THE COMPUTER

One of the best ways to beat the computer is to play a light-and-sound game. *Touch Me* by Atari, for example, offers three different games. When you turn it on, the computer flashes a light or plays a musical note. You have to repeat it eight, sixteen, thirty-two, or ninety-nine times—depending on how sharp you feel. If you win, the computer surrenders like a good sport and treats you to a light-and-sound show. When you get tired playing the computer, you can play a friend.

NUMBER CRUNCHERS

If you are more math-oriented (or would like to be), try one of the many number-crunching games available. You can program a math problem (like the addition of two huge numbers) into the computer. You sit down and figure out the problem yourself and key in your answer. If you are right, the computer flashes a green light. If you're wrong, the computer buzzes at you and blinks a red light.

COMP IV by Milton Bradley and *Digits* by Coleco are two especially exciting number-cruncher games. Both let you play detective and track down a three-, four-, or five-digit number they have hidden in memory.

A game computer like Milton Bradley's *COMP IV* is especially tough to beat because its brain never gets tired. It's got thousands and thousands of numbers for you to guess—one right after another. How can you outwit it? Pay attention to the clues it gives you. [Courtesy of Milton Bradley Company.]

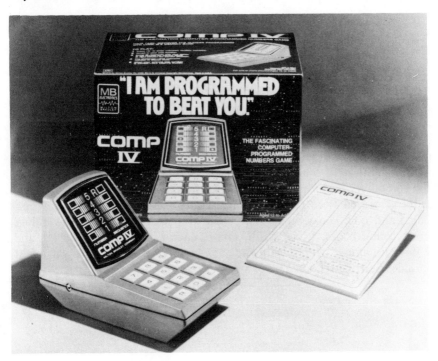

Like Sherlock Holmes solving a crime, you have to use logic and deduction to pin down the right number. Then another number. And another . . . and another. *COMP IV* alone can come up with more than thirty thousand different numbers for you to guess.

WORD SCRAMBLERS

Do you like to play word games? One of the most grueling is *Brain Baffler* by Mattel. *Brain Baffler* plays a variety of games, has a time clock to keep you on your toes, and has several sound effects. Its games include *Go Hang*, *Mixed-Up Words*, *Build-A-Word*, *Flash Word*, and *Third-Degree Anagrams*. In *Flash Word*, for example, the computer comes up with eight random letters. Every four seconds a letter changes. If you see a word hidden in the letters, you punch a button to freeze the letters on the screen. You've got thirty seconds to type in the word you see. If you are right, the computer cheers and rewards you with game points. If you're wrong, you get buzzed.

If you like to play detective and track down words instead of criminals, you'll love *Hangman*. In this game, you try to guess a missing word, one letter at a time. At the beginning all you know is how many letters there are in the word. Every time you miss a letter, the computer adds a piece to a hanging figure on the display. If you guess too many wrong letters, the little fellow's figure is completed, he gets hanged, and you lose.

KNOW-IT-ALL

Anyone ever call you a "walking encyclopedia?" They will, after you've beaten the computer quiz games. One of these, *Quiz Wiz* by Coleco, is especially difficult because of the large number of categories and questions stored on it.

To play *Quiz Wiz*, you plug a game cartridge into the computer, choose a question from the quiz book, pick one of the numbered answers, and push the right button on the computer. If you get the right answer, the computer "beeps" and flashes a green light. If you're wrong, the computer gives you the "raspberry" and flashes a red light. There are cartridges and quiz books on sports, people and places, disasters, how things work, comic books, trivia, math, music, energy, the oceans, movies, and TV—you name it. If you learn the answers to all the questions you might consider quitting school. You're a genius!

A computer game like *Quiz Wiz* from Coleco is especially good because it's open-ended: Its questions (on each subject—like "Energy" or "How Things Work") are stored on preprogrammed game cartridge. Whenever you get tired of a subject, just pop out the cartridge and plug in a new one. [Courtesy of Coleco Industries, Inc.]

TINY VIDEO

Let's say it's summertime, and you are looking for a job. Right now you're at the city's youth employment office, standing in line. There must be forty people ahead of you. You'll be here all morning. What to do? In your brain a light bulb comes on. You reach inside your knapsack and pull out your *Microvision* computer.

Microvision, by Milton Bradley, has its own tiny video screen along with several different programs. You start by playing *Blockbuster*, where you knock down a wall of bricks to escape from jail. You go *Bowling*, then play *Pinball*. You look up: You're still way back in line. You play several games of *Vegas Slots* and try to beat the computer one-arm bandit. Then you blast off into outer space and play *Star Trek Phaser Strike*. Again, you look up. There are only a few people left ahead of you. You've got just enough time for *Mindbuster,* a logic puzzle game. You're wrestling with one of the puzzles when you hear a voice from far off say, "Next." You look up. You made it. It's your turn!

SOLVE A CRIME

You are a big-city detective walking along a block in a dangerous part of town. Somewhere on the block a crime is committed by an invisible thief. It's up to you to track him down and get the cops to arrest him. That sets the stage for Parker Brothers' crimefighter game, *Stop Thief®.*

A game like Parker Brothers' *Stop Thief*® is a combination board game and computer game. Board games in the future will be played on a large, flat computer screen built into a table. You will move, throw dice, and draw cards simply by touching a game "menu" with your finger. [*Stop Thief*® game equipment © 1979 Parker Brothers, Beverly, MA 01915. Used by permission.]

You play the game on a regular game board. But there's a computer Crime Scanner to give you clues in the form of suspicious noises—creaking doors, breaking glass, creepy footsteps, sirens, and gunshots. If you're lucky and catch the thief, you call the police, and the Crime Scanner makes the sound of a squad car rolling up, with its siren on full blast. But be careful! Before the police arrive, the clever thief is liable to give you the slip.

Another dramatic crimefighter game is *Electronic Detective* by Ideal. The computer is an evil criminal genius. It dares you to guess who committed a murder. If you guess wrong—BANG!!—you're out of the game. If nobody nails the killer, the computer plays funeral music and ends the game. You've got your work cut out for you: The computer mastermind has 130,000 different crimes in its memory.

CAPTURE
A KING

*When I saw the knight sacrificed in the first game, and the
follow-up move, my first reaction was, "This is dreadful—the
thing is beating me!"*

The person who made this remark is David Levy, an international chess
grandmaster. The "thing" he is referring to is a chess-playing computer.
Levy made the remark in Toronto during a match that pitted him against
CHESS 4.7, an advanced chess program.

Before the match, Levy seemed confident. "It's a struggle between
man and machine," he said. "Personally, I think I will destroy it." After
the match, Levy was happy to have escaped with a victory. He had won
three games, but the computer had taken one game, and in another,
played Levy to a draw. Levy now predicts that within five years he will be
beaten by a chess program. In fact, he and *Omni* magazine are offering a
joint prize of five thousand dollars for the first computer to beat him.

The current world-champion chess program is the *DUCHESS*, developed by students at Duke University in Durham, North Carolina. Perhaps *DUCHESS* will be the first computer program to beat David Levy
and claim his five thousand dollar prize.

Computer programs that can beat grandmasters do not run on home
computers—yet. They require huge quantities of memory and several million calculations a second. Only a giant computer can provide this. On
the other hand, there are several respectable chess programs that run on
home computers. Perhaps the best-known is SARGON, the winner of the
chess tournament at the 1978 West Coast Computer Faire. You can load
SARGON on your home computer by typing the program listing found

DUCHESS, the chess-playing program from Duke University, analyzes one and a half million moves to counter just one of your moves. It has a "personality," too: It favors some openings and options more than others, and it tries to bluff you by claiming it is in a better position than it really is. [Courtesy of the *Daily Tar Heel*, Chapel Hill, NC. Photo by Will Owens.]

in the *SARGON* book, or you can buy a tape cassette with the program already on it.

If you like to play chess, and you haven't played a chess computer yet, get ready for a treat: There are also several hand-held chess computers available. They are tough, easy to operate, and are surprisingly "human."

Recently, in New York's famed Marshall Chess Club, *Popular Mechanics* magazine sponsored a computer chess tournament and let the little electronic grandmasters go at it. Chess master Shelby Lyman moderated. At the end of seventy-five hours of exhausting play, *Chess Challenger* 10 from Fidelity Electronics was declared the hands-down winner. Making a respectable showing were *Boris* from Chafitz, Inc., *CompuChess* from DataCash, and *Chess Champion* from JS&A.

Many people think that the winner, *Chess Challenger* 10, is so good it deserves a U. S. Chess Federation rating. It is estimated that *Challenger*—set at its highest playing level—could beat 90 per cent of the forty million Americans who play chess.

Although *Challenger* is possibly the best chess-playing computer, *Boris* is the most human. In its (ROM) memory it has eighty different comments to throw at you during a game, including "Hurray!," "I need help," and "Ah, ruthless."

All of the computers make excellent chess teachers and chess-playing companions. They play at different levels of skill and help you build your confidence and playing ability. They have special features, too. *Challenger* will "beep" at you when it's your turn. *Boris* displays little pictures of the chessmen to show where they are on the board. Also, *Boris* has a timer to adjust his "move" time from one second to one hundred hours. As you would expect, he gets smarter and smarter the more time you give him. Maybe the best feature of all about chess-playing computers is that you can trust them not to tell anyone when you lose an easy game.

ESCAPE
FROM
A MAZE

Remember Theseus? He was the Greek hero made prisoner in the Labyrinth, a horrible dungeon of mazelike passages under the island of Crete. Being stuck in the Labyrinth was bad enough. But Theseus had company—the Minotaur, a ferocious creature, half bull and half man.

Can you escape from a maze? You can pretend you're Theseus and fight your way past Minotaurs, dragons, and Wumpuses to get past mazes built by the tricky computer. You can write your own maze programs complete with dead ends and monsters, you can buy canned maze games, or you can try one of the hand-held maze games already on the market. One of these, *Amaze-a-Tron* by Coleco, is a maze game for people who've never gotten lost in a maze before. It features a relatively simple maze with no monster. The computer tells you the starting point where you are trapped, and points out an exit at the other end of the maze. Your job is to work your way toward the exit. If you go in the right direction, the computer plays a tune to reward you. If you bump into a maze "wall," you get razzed. If you get out and are still fresh, tell the computer you want a new maze—it's got a million!

Among the canned maze games look for *Caves, Snark, Hurkle,* and *Mugwump.* And there is *Wumpus,* which features a crazy maze of rooms in the shape of a *dodecahedron* (a twelve-sided, three-dimensional figure). Somewhere inside the maze, a huge, ugly Wumpus is sleeping— sleeping, that is, until you wake him up. Then, CHOMP! He eats you. So, "Shhh." Be quiet and try to escape from the maze without waking the Wumpus. And on the way out, watch out for the Bottomless Pits, and for the Super Bats who might pick you up and drop you Somewhere Else.

If, by chance, you escape from the Wumpus, try escaping from a maze on one of the "wizard" computers. They have monsters and 3-D labyrinths that are set up like a movie: You see the maze from the inside just as if you were actually there. This alone is exciting. But wait until you turn a corner and find a thirty-foot dragon waiting for you!

BEWARE
OF DRAGONS

The news clipping on the next page is fictitious, but the story is true. A student from the university did actually disappear into the underground pipes. As for the young man himself, he eventually turned up in another state, safe and unharmed. He had gotten tired of playing the game in the steam pipes, and decided to run away from home.

This particular fellow received a lot of attention because of his disappearance, but he is not alone. There are hundreds of thousands of young people across the United States frantically playing this new kind of computer game—the *Epic Fantasy Game*. They are so single-mindedly devoted that they sometimes play a single game nonstop several days in a row.

There are dozens of these games to choose from, with versions for all the major home computers. The games combine the action and suspense of a good mystery novel, with the mental challenge of a game of chess.

The games are all *simulations*, or *models*, of fantasy worlds full of glittering treasures and creatures who are horrible and evil. When you play a game, you become the central character, the hero. You always have a goal or mission. Depending on the game, you need to find a lost treasure, rescue a princess, or simply escape from the dangers that surround you.

An Epic Fantasy Game is so fascinating—and so popular—for many reasons:

First, and most important, the game is exciting because you are the chief character—the space pilot, the explorer, the knight-errant. It is impossible to get detached and grow bored when you are the one who earns

MISSING!

East Lansing, Mich. (CP)— Last night, police informed reporters that a sixteen-year-old MSU student is missing from his college dormitory. He was last seen exploring the steam pipes underneath the university campus. The boy used the pipes to act out scenes from the Dungeons & Dragons® game he played on a computer. Police fear that the youth is lost somewhere in the maze of underground tunnels.

Friends of the youth said that the computer game was so realis-

"DUNGEONS & DRAGONS is a registered trademark owned by TSR Hobbies, Inc."

the rewards, when you are the one who single-handedly faces danger, the threat of injury, even death.

Second, an Epic Fantasy Game is complicated and challenging. Don't expect to play one and win the very first time. The game begins, and the world you enter is a vast and menacing wilderness full of mazes, caves, and enchanted forests. It might take you hours just to explore the world, much less master it.

Third, an Epic Fantasy Game is surprising and unpredictable, so you never know what's going to happen next. At any moment, you might be ambushed by a troll, attacked by a dragon, swallowed by a pit—or you might discover a priceless treasure.

Fourth, although the games are based in part on chance, they are also games of skill. To win a game—to find the treasure, earn a winning number of points, or get out alive—you need to be sharp. If you aren't alert, you will miss the opportunities that come your way: the ax you need to defend yourself; the water you need to survive; or the lamp you need to light your way. Instead, you will waste time wandering down cave passages you've already explored, and stumble into castle chambers inhabited by ferocious monsters.

Epic Fantasy Games seem so real because of the danger, the challenge, the suspense, and the adventure that *you* experience each time you play. [Courtesy of the *Daily Tar Heel*, Chapel Hill, NC. Photo by Mark Murrell.]

Fifth, an Epic Fantasy Game rarely turns out the same way each time you play it. You can play again and again, and still be challenged, puzzled, and stymied by the clever villains, the awesome, crumbling cliffs, and the other unexpected obstacles the computer places in your path.

Sixth, the computer has a pretty large vocabulary. As you play the game and talk to the computer, the illusion grows that the computer is a person and that the world inside the computer is real.

Last, an Epic Fantasy Game is exciting because you play it exactly at your own speed. If you are thoughtful and cautious, the computer is patient. But if you are fearless and bold—even foolish—the computer lets you race through the game, confronting danger on the run.

MAKE A
MILLION
DOLLARS

STAR TRADER

The date is January 1, 2070. Interstellar flight has existed for seventy years. There are several star systems that have been colonized. Some are only frontier systems, others are older and more developed.

You are captain of two interstellar trading ships. You travel from one star system to another, buying and selling merchandise. If you drive a hard bargain, you can make huge profits.

Star Trader is one of many *business simulation games*—games in which you play the part of a business person or merchant.* For example, in *Star Trader*, you start the game with five thousand Interplanetary Dollars. It is up to you to whiz around the galaxy in your spaceship, closing deals, trading goods, and making money. If you love to gamble and speculate, then you will find these games intriguing and fascinating.

Games like *Star Trader*, in spite of their science-fiction, fantasylike, or historical setting, help you learn many of the basics about handling money. They teach you how to make investments, buy and sell goods and services, and pay debts. They teach you how to distinguish a good deal from a bad one; how to stretch a tight budget; and how to become a

---

* This is a variation of the *Star Trader* game in *What to Do After You Hit Return*, published by People's Computer Company (Menlo Park, Calif., 1975), pp. 94–97.

STAR MAP

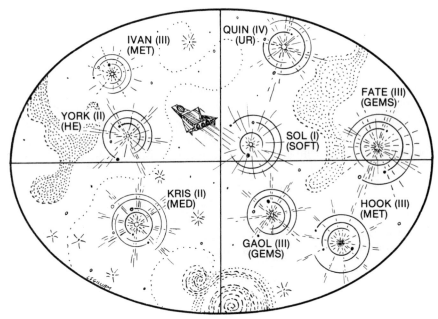

(The map is 100 light years by 140 light years)

STAR-SYSTEM CLASSES	MERCHANDISE	
I Cosmopolitan	UR	Uranium
II Developed	MET	Metals
III Underdeveloped	HE	Heavy Equipment
IV Frontier	MED	Medicine
	SOFT	Computer Software
	GEMS	Star Gems

tough and canny bargainer. Since you are dealing in swiftly changing amounts of money, these games also sharpen your math skills. There are many good business-simulation games, like:

HAMURABI You are the ancient Babylonian ruler Hammurabi. You need to manage your kingdom's agricultural economy skillfully in order to feed your people. There is always the threat of plagues and starvation.

KING Like *Hamurabi*, but more difficult and challenging. Now you must also educate your people and deal with pollution. If you fail, you face jail, hanging, or assassination.

MARKET You and your friends are the managers of competing corporations. You choose the product. Each business quarter, you make decisions about production, advertising, the price of your product, sales, profits, and cash on hand. To win, you must raise your company's assets to twelve million dollars. Watch out! It's easy to lose a fortune and have your company go bankrupt.

STOCK Play the stock market. You start with ten thousand dollars. It's up to you to choose stocks that go up and not down. Invest your money cautiously—or speculatively. It's up to you. At any point in the game, you can see where you stand by printing the names of your stocks, their current prices, and the number of shares in your portfolio. Be careful. At any moment, the market might crash and leave you without a dime.

TAIPEI You are a Western merchant in China in the late 1800s. At first, you deal in general goods. Then, as your fortunes mount, you graduate to arms and silk—and, ultimately, to the deadly narcotic, opium. Your business deals are complicated by questions of morality and ethics, by rumors and threats, and by constant intrigue.

INVENT YOUR OWN GAMES

I f you're the creative type and you find yourself growing bored with even the fanciest canned games, by all means invent one of your own! Designing your own game is tricky at first, but it's not difficult. And it can be a lot of fun. Here are some of the ground rules:

First, outline your game before starting to write the program. Make sure you know exactly how you want the game to work. How can you be certain that your game is exciting and fun to play? Include these six sure-fire elements of a good game: *realism, action, suspense, luck, strategy,* and *surprise.*

Second, get familiar with all the commands in your computer's programming language. You are going to need every one of them to make a good game.

Third, pay special attention to game-oriented commands that produce tones, sound, and music (like the "PEEK," "POKE," and "CALL SOUND" commands in *BASIC*); also to commands (like "SET-COLOR") that produce color pictures; and commands (like "RAN-DOMIZE" and "RND") that add the element of luck to your game.*

Fourth, pretend you are the computer, ask the questions the computer will ask the game players, and print the messages the computer will display on the screen.

* See chapters titled "You're Trapped!," "Play an Orchestra," and "Paint a Picture" to see how these commands are used in real programs.

Fifth, get some graph paper (with little square blocks) and "X" the pictures you want your game to draw on the TV screen. Then look at how the programming language divides the screen up into *pixels* "picture elements"—rows and columns of dots or boxes. Before you try to draw complicated game pictures of dragons, mazes, and spaceships, you should play around with simpler programs that just draw lines and boxes on different parts of the screen. Change the color of the dots. Make them beep and buzz. Make them move!

Sixth, write out the main commands your program will need to introduce itself, send messages, draw pictures, keep scores, calculate odds, send insults, and say good-by. Remember, do the important jobs first and worry about the details later—one at a time.

Seventh, write the entire program, section by section, task by task. Remember, your game players are only human. They may sometimes enter the wrong answers to the computer's questions. It might even be such an unpredictable answer that your program won't know what to do, and it will just stop working, or *crash.* You'd better play it safe and add *error traps* that make your program catch these unexpected answers, flash the game player a message like "Wrong Answer—Try Again, Please," and then loop back to ask the same question again.

Eighth and last, test your game on the computer. Get ready to spend hours and hours chasing down bugs that are so sneaky you begin to believe your computer is inhabited by gremlins and ghosts. Then be prepared to spend more hours fussing and fuming over the game, trying to make it faster, trickier, and more fun.

If you find yourself enjoying all this, keep it in the back of your mind that someday you might come up with a game that's so spectacular you could sell it to other home-computer owners. It might even be good enough to interest a home-computer company, a software (canned-program) company, or a game manufacturer like Mattel or Milton Bradley. Game designers are interested in learning about new games that would be a hit with the hundreds of thousands of people who play games on home computers.

YOU'RE
TRAPPED!

Y ou are a cave explorer inside an enormous cavern deep under the
earth. A section of the cavern's roof crashes behind you, blocking
your way out. *You're* Trapped!

But wait: In front of you are six passages—tiny corridors through
unimaginable tons of stone. You remember now: One of these passages
leads up and out of the cave. The others all end in solid rock—dead ends.
You have no food and little water. Which is the right passage? You have
to decide quickly.

THE COMPUTER GAME

You sit down at the computer, turn it on, enter the "TRAPPED!"
program into the computer's memory—by typing it in, or by loading a
tape cassette or floppy. To get the program to *execute*, you type "RUN."
The computer answers:

TRAPPED!
* * * * * * *

YOU ARE IN AN ENORMOUS CAVERN
UNDERNEATH COUNTLESS TONS OF
SOLID ROCK.

THE WAY YOU ENTERED THE CAVERN
HAS BEEN BLOCKED OFF. THERE ARE
SIX UNEXPLORED PASSAGES DIRECTLY

IN FRONT OF YOU. ONLY ONE LEADS
OUT OF THE CAVERN.

```
XXXXXXXXXXXXXXXXXXXXXXXXXXXXXXXXXXXXXXXXX
XXXXX   XXX   XXX   XXX   XXX   XXX   XXXXX
XXXXX 1 XXX 2 XXX 3 XXX 4 XXX 5 XXX 6 XXXXX
XXXXX   XXX   XXX   XXX   XXX   XXX   XXXXX
XXXXXXXXXXXXXXXXXXXXXXXXXXXXXXXXXXXXXXXXX
```

WHICH PASSAGE WILL YOU EXPLORE (1–6)?

Confidently, you type a "3" for passage No. 3. The computer answers:

YOU ARE WALKING ALONG CAVE PASSAGE 3 . . .
    WALKING . . .
    WALKING . . .
    WALKING . . .
YOU SEE BATS . . . YOU HEAR EERIE NOISES . . .
    WALKING . . .
    WALKING . . .
    WALKING . . .

A DEAD END!! YOU MUST GO BACK!!
YOUR WATER IS RUNNING LOW.
QUICK, WHAT NEW PASSAGE DO YOU CHOOSE?

Less confidently, you type a "1" for passage No. 1. Uh-oh! Same message! You try a "6," then a "4." You're still trapped! You feel yourself getting thirsty. You're growing weaker. The air is getting bad. Your hand shakes as you type a "2" for passage No. 2. The computer answers:

YOU ARE WALKING ALONG CAVE PASSAGE 2 . . .
    WALKING . . .
    WALKING . . .
    WALKING . . .
YOU SEE BATS . . . YOU HEAR EERIE NOISES . . .
    WALKING . . .
    WALKING . . .
    WALKING . . .

SUNLIGHT!! YOU MADE IT!!
YOU FOUND THE WAY OUT!!
DO YOU DARE GO BACK INSIDE THE CAVE (Y/N)?

You smile with relief, then shake your head and type an "N" for no. You turn off the computer and run to the kitchen for a tall glass of water.

THE PROGRAM'S MAJOR TASKS

The program "TRAPPED!" is a *game of chance:* Each time you play, the computer randomly chooses a new number for the cave passage that leads out of the cave. You don't know which number it's going to be: No. 1, No. 2, No. 3, No. 4, No. 5, or No. 6.

Before you look at the "TRAPPED!" program and begin learning each command, make a list of the program's main tasks:

1. the program must introduce itself. This identifies the program and gives you some information about the game.

2. at the beginning of each game the program picks a new set of six passages: five dead ends and one exit from the cavern.

3. the program asks you to pick a cave passage.

4. you choose a passage, and the program compares your choice with the passage it has chosen as the real exit.

5. if the two passages match, the computer prints a message: You

have escaped! Then it asks if you want to play again. If you say yes, the computer loops back to No. 2. If you say no, it jumps to No. 7.

6. if the passages don't match, the computer prints another message: dead end! It asks you what passage you choose next. Then it loops back to No. 4.

7. the program ends.

THE FLOW CHART FOR *TRAPPED!*

Now that you have a list of the program's seven major tasks, you need to see how they fit together. To do that, you convert the list into a program *flow chart*—a diagram showing how the program is supposed to work.

Flowchart of TRAPPED!
(A Cave Adventure Game Based on Chance)

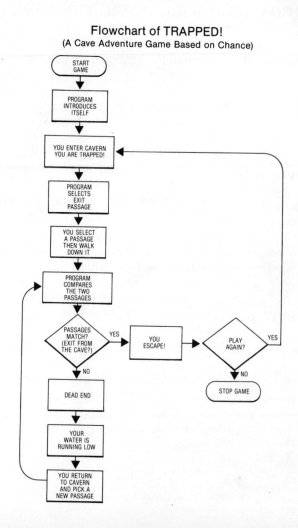

THE PROGRAM

"TRAPPED!" is written in *BASIC*. Here is the actual program:

```
10 PRINT
20 PRINT "          TRAPPED!"
30 PRINT "          ********"
40 PRINT
50 GOSUB 820
60 PRINT "YOU ARE IN AN ENORMOUS CAVERN"
70 PRINT "UNDERNEATH COUNTLESS TONS OF"
80 PRINT "SOLID ROCK."
90 PRINT
100 PRINT "THE WAY YOU ENTERED THE CAVERN"
110 PRINT "HAS BEEN BLOCKED OFF.  THERE ARE"
120 PRINT "SIX UNEXPLORED PASSAGES DIRECTLY"
130 PRINT "IN FRONT OF YOU.  ONLY ONE LEADS"
140 PRINT "OUT OF THE CAVERN."
150 PRINT
160 PRINT "XXXXXXXXXXXXXXXXXXXXXXXXXXXXXXXXXXXXXXXXXXXXXXXXXXXXXXXX"
170 PRINT "XXXXX     XXX      XXX      XXX      XXX      XXX   XXXX"
180 PRINT "XXXXX  1  XXX  2   XXX  3   XXX  4   XXX  5   XXX  6 XXXX"
190 PRINT "XXXXX     XXX      XXX      XXX      XXX      XXX   XXXX"
200 PRINT "XXXXXXXXXXXXXXXXXXXXXXXXXXXXXXXXXXXXXXXXXXXXXXXXXXXXXXXX"
210 PRINT
220 FOR I = 1 TO 6
230 GOSUB 820
240 NEXT I
250 RANDOMIZE
260 LET A = INT(6 * RND(1) + 1)
270 PRINT "WHICH PASSAGE WILL YOU EXPLORE (1 - 6)?"
280 INPUT B
290 PRINT
300 PRINT
310 GOSUB 820
320 PRINT "YOU ARE WALKING ALONG CAVE PASSAGE";
330 PRINT B;
340 PRINT "... "
350 PRINT
360 PRINT
370 FOR I = 1 TO 3
380 GOSUB 820
390 PRINT "  WALKING ..."
400 PRINT
410 NEXT I
420 PRINT
430 GOSUB 820
440 PRINT "YOU SEE BATS  ... YOU HEAR EERIE NOISES ... "
450 PRINT
460 GOSUB 820
470 FOR I = 1 TO 3
480 GOSUB 820
490 PRINT "  WALKING ..."
500 PRINT
510 NEXT I
520 PRINT
530 GOSUB 820
540 IF A = B GOTO 620
550 PRINT "A DEAD END!!  YOU MUST GO BACK!!"
560 PRINT
570 GOSUB 820
580 PRINT "YOUR WATER IS RUNNING LOW."
590 PRINT
600 PRINT "QUICK, WHAT NEW PASSAGE DO YOU CHOOSE?"
610 GOTO 280
620 PRINT
630 PRINT "SUNLIGHT!!  YOU MADE IT!!"
640 PRINT
650 GOSUB 820
660 PRINT "YOU FOUND THE WAY OUT!!"
670 PRINT
680 PRINT "DO YOU DARE GO BACK INSIDE THE CAVE? (Y/N)"
690 INPUT C$
700 IF C$ = "N" OR C$ = "NO" GOTO 760
710 PRINT
720 PRINT
730 GOSUB 820
740 PRINT "ONCE AGAIN, ";
750 GOTO 60
760 PRINT
770 GOSUB 820
780 PRINT "GOOD IDEA ... MAYBE LATER ..."
790 PRINT
800 GOSUB 820
810 END
820 FOR J = 1 TO 500:NEXT J
830 RETURN
```

Left margin annotations:

Program introduces itself

You enter the cavern. You are trapped

You choose a passage / Program selects exit passage / Pause

Walking along passage

Is this the exit passage?

Wrong passage: dead end!

Right passage: you escape!

Play again?

Yes

No

"Pause" subroutine

THE TEN COMMANDS

There are ten major commands that appear in the program. The *line numbers* tell the *BASIC* interpreter the order in which the commands should be obeyed. The numbers are spaced ten apart in case you need to add new commands in between the old ones. Here are the ten commands:

1. RANDOMIZE and RND
2. PRINT
3. LET
4. INPUT
5. IF
6. GOTO and GOSUB
7. FOR . . . NEXT
8. END
9. NEW
10. RUN

COMMAND NO. 1: RANDOMIZE and RND

These commands convert the "TRAPPED!" program into a game of chance.

COMMAND NO. 2: PRINT

The "PRINT" command (line 10 on) tells the *BASIC* interpreter to send the message contained in double quotes (") to the *output device* (the video terminal, typewriter, etc.). If no message follows the "PRINT" command, the interpreter sends a *blank line* to the output device.

COMMAND NO. 3: LET

The "LET" command sets up a storage location, an *address*, in the computer's main memory—its RAM. Then it stores data in that address.

COMMAND NO. 4: INPUT

The "INPUT" command (on lines 280 and 690) tells the *BASIC* interpreter to print a question mark (?) and then read in whatever you type on the *input device* (video terminal, typewriter, etc.). From then on, the "INPUT" command functions like the "LET" command: It tells the interpreter to store the data it reads in at an address in RAM.

COMMAND NO. 5:   IF

The "IF" command (on lines 540 and 700) enables the program to *make decisions*. If a condition is true ("IF A=B"), then the interpreter performs the rest of the command. In both cases in the program, the rest of the command is a *"jump"* to another part of the program. If the condition is not true, the interpreter ignores the rest of the command and goes to the command on the next line.

COMMAND NO. 6:   GOTO and GOSUB

Unless told to do otherwise, the interpreter normally runs a program by sending one command at a time to the CPU for processing—starting with the lowest line number and ending with the highest. The "GOTO" and "GOSUB" commands cause the CPU to jump forward—or backward —to the specified line number. When the CPU encounters a "RE-TURN" after a "GOSUB," it boomerangs back to the next line following the "GOSUB." But watch out! If you use too many "GOTOs," your program's flow chart looks like a plate of spaghetti noodles, with loops and arrows crisscrossing wildly up and down the page. Worse, when the poor computer tries to run the program, it bounces around like a hyperactive kangaroo.

COMMAND NO. 7:   FOR . . . NEXT

A program is in a *loop* when it does the same commands over and over. Two "GOTO" commands will produce a loop, but the "FOR . . . NEXT" commands (on lines 220, 370, 470, and 820) are especially designed for looping, so they make an excellent substitute for a "GOTO" command. The "FOR" command begins a loop and sets the number of times the loop is to take place. The "NEXT" command resets the *loop counter*, "I," acts as the end of the loop, and also acts as an implicit "GOTO" back to the top of the loop. Each time the loop is completed, an automatic check is made to see if the loop counter is greater than the number of loops desired. If it is, the interpreter jumps to the command that follows the "NEXT" command.

COMMAND NO. 8: END

This command "ENDs" your program. When the interpreter sees this command, it stops sending program commands to the CPU for processing, and it tells you it is "READY" for another program 'or for *system* (file handling) commands.

COMMAND NO. 9: NEW

This command never appears inside a program: It is a *system command*. Each time you use *BASIC*, the interpreter reserves a section of RAM for your programs—one program at a time. This storage space is known as a *program work area*. NEW cleans the work area of stray data and commands, or *garbage*.

COMMAND NO. 10: RUN

This is the most important system command. It tells the *BASIC* interpreter to take each command stored in the work area, translate it into machine language, then send it to the CPU for processing. This is the command that makes your computer "come alive."

EXPERIMENTING WITH YOUR PROGRAM

"TRAPPED!" is short and simple, and has no fancy bells and whistles. But it doesn't have to stay that way. It's *your* program now: Add to it, change it, make it more challenging, exciting—and more reliable.

To make the "TRAPPED!" program more *reliable*, add error traps—tests to catch mistakes in people's answers to the computer. For example, when the computer asks, "WHICH PASSAGE WILL YOU EXPLORE (1–6)?" what if the person answered, "7," or, maybe, "X"?

Also, to make the program easier to understand, add *comments* that explain the program's major tasks. Just write up the comments, decide where you want to put them, and type each one into the work area preceded by a line number and a "REM" command (for "remark").

How about making the program *more challenging?* For example, the program just types, "YOUR WATER IS RUNNING LOW." You never know how much water you have or how much you use when you stumble down a wrong passage. Why not make the poor, trapped cave explorer even more nervous by gradually draining his water supply, then telling him how little he has left?

Can you make the program *more exciting?* How about dangerous cave creatures lurking among dark, slimy passages? How about bottomless pits, falling rocks, and cave-ins? You could dream up a different peril in every passage, waiting—silently waiting—for the hapless explorer to come tramping by.

GETTING STARTED

This was just a brief sample of what it takes to write a game program. If you're anxious to begin inventing your own games, now's the time to read a *programming manual* written especially for the home computer you are using. It will tell you exactly what *BASIC* commands your computer uses, in case they're different from what you learned here. Also, there are many excellent books that teach you how to write programs in *BASIC*—and in the other popular home computer languages like *PAS-CAL, PILDT, APL,* and *PL/M.* (Take a look at the list of books recommended in Appendix A.) The purpose of this section was just to get you started. With a little practice and a little more learning, you'll soon be inventing games on your own.

PROJECTS

BUILD
A ROBOT

Just a few years ago, robots were the stuff of science fiction—creatures of fantasy and the far-off future. Not so any longer. Thanks to tiny computers, space-age metals, and lightweight plastics, the robots are coming. In fact, they are already here.

ROBERT AND SB-3400

Robert Profeta is a high-school student who lives in Vineland, New Jersey. He is currently working on his fourth robot.

Robert's latest model is called *Mars Lunar Rover Robot SB-3400*. Robert made SB-3400 out of a big tin can, a plastic globe, spray paint, plywood, little DC motors, and a twelve-volt motorcycle battery, among other things. What can SB-3400 do? It can tell you the temperature (and sound an alarm when it gets too hot or too cold), detect contaminated water, give a nervous friend a lie-detector test, talk to you, and bring you a glass of water. Robert runs SB-3400 using a control box and a long extension cord.

Robert is already at work on the successor to SB-3400, which he calls *DC Prober*. *Prober* has longer arms to extend its reach and make it more useful. It is also more powerful: Robert can climb on *Prober* and go for a ride.

Robert is one of many young inventors around the United States (and the world) who are building their own robots. Nevertheless, although there are thousands of robots working in factories, it is still unusual to have one around the house. But that's changing. The invention of new, durable lightweight plastics, the advances in robot technology made in NASA's unmanned space probes, and the development of miniature

Robert Profeta of Vineland, New Jersey, and *SB-3400,* one of several robots he has built in his own home. Robert often takes his robots to conventions. Once when he was demonstrating how one of his robots could lift a cup, people thought the robot was looking for a handout and tossed coins into the cup.

computer-brain and memory circuits have put robots on your doorstep.

Robert's robots do not have a computer "brain." They are run by remote control—by extension cords and radio signals from a hand-held control box. Since they have no computer, the robots can't be programmed to run on their own. On the other hand, since they have no computer, the robots are easier to build. Robert builds his on the kitchen floor of his family's apartment.

TOD AND *MIKE*

One of the robot inventors who is using computers is Tod Loofbourrow. Tod built a computer-controlled robot named *Mike* (for *Microtron*). *Mike* can be independent and explore Tod's home on his own, or he can be operated by remote control like Robert's robots. *Mike* runs on three wheels at two different speeds, and is strong enough to push or pull 150 pounds, or carry over 600 pounds. *Mike* knows where he is going because

Tod Loofbourrow of Westfield, New Jersey, and his computer-controlled robot *Mike*. When Tod finishes with him, *Mike* will be about five feet tall, have mechanical arms, be able to talk, and have a video terminal on his chest so Tod can reprogram him. [Photo courtesy of Tod Loofbourrow.]

the position of his wheels sends electric charges to an A–D (*analog-to-digital*) *converter* that transforms the charges into *digital signals* that are sent directly to *Mike*'s CPU brain for processing.*

Mike can also see where he is going thanks to an on-board *ultrasonic transducer*. This device sends a signal made of extremely high-pitched sound waves inaudible to the human ear. The signal is sent every quarter of a second, bounces off the nearest object, and returns to *Mike*. *Mike* calculates the distance to the object based on the time it takes for the signal to return. He calculates the position and distance of an object all in a fraction of a second. He adjusts his direction and speed accordingly, in order to avoid the object.

Mike also has an *impact sensor* and *soft rubber feelers* mounted only two inches off the floor. If his ultrasonic "eyes" miss an object, he will gently bump into it, "notice" it, and instantly back away.

An on-board microphone gives *Mike* his "ears." When he "hears" a command, he checks a *command table* in his memory. A command table is a list of English-language commands followed by the machine-language instructions that enable *Mike* to obey the command. If a command is in the command table, *Mike* instantly obeys it. In this way, Tod can control *Mike* from a distance just by talking to him. He can tell *Mike* to move forward, move backward, go faster, turn right, turn left, or stop. Tod can also adjust *Mike*'s *voice-recognition program* so that *Mike* recognizes him and no one else.

Is *Mike* complete the way he is now? Tod says no. He plans to make many improvements to *Mike* over the near future. First, Tod wants to add a five-foot body to *Mike* that includes a video terminal, keyboard, and some arms so *Mike* can pick up things and carry them. Next, Tod plans to give *Mike* the ability to talk. *Mike* will store a vocabulary of several hundred words in his memory. When he is called upon to say something, *Mike* will fetch each word from memory. Then he will convert each word from a digital to an analog signal using a D–A (*digital-to-analog*) *converter*. The new signal will represent sound waves in the form of electrical charges. The charges will be sent to a speaker, where they are transformed into actual sounds—*Mike*'s "voice."

Mike's next major improvement will be an *image sensor* (or video)

---

* Home computers use digital signals—voltages that are on or off, high or low—to store and process information. But things in the real world rarely are just on or off, high or low. For example, *Mike*'s wheels are circles, each with an infinite number of points. When one of these wheels turns, it generates an electrical *analog* signal exactly equal to the portion of the circle actually turned. But *Mike* can't process that signal because it's not on or off, high or low—it's somewhere in between. That's where the A–D (analog-to-digital) converter comes in. It translates the exact, *analog* signal to a *digital* (high-low) signal that approximates the portion of the circle that was turned. Once the information has been *digitized*, *Mike* can store it and process it.

camera. This will enable *Mike* to "see" objects using light waves instead of ultrasonic sound waves. The visual images that the camera captures will be converted into digital signals and matched against other images stored in memory in a *visual-image command table* similar to *Mike's* voice-recognition command table.

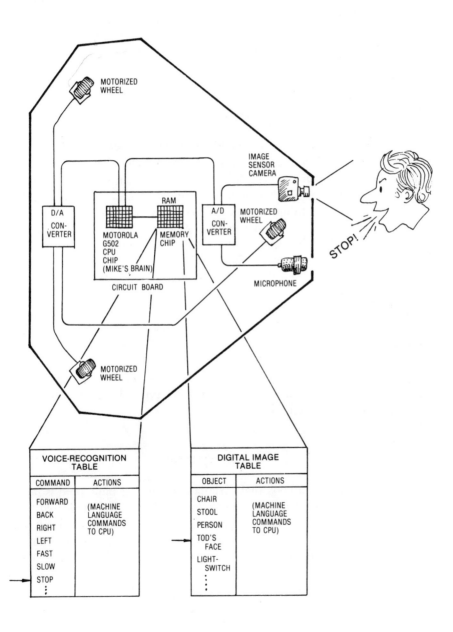

VOICE-RECOGNITION TABLE	
COMMAND	ACTIONS
FORWARD	(MACHINE
BACK	LANGUAGE
RIGHT	COMMANDS
LEFT	TO CPU)
FAST	
SLOW	
STOP	
⋮	

DIGITAL IMAGE TABLE	
OBJECT	ACTIONS
CHAIR	(MACHINE
STOOL	LANGUAGE
PERSON	COMMANDS
TOD'S FACE	TO CPU)
LIGHT-SWITCH	
⋮	

MIKE IN ACTION

Let's see what all this equipment might allow *Mike* to do. Let's say it's 9 P.M. at Tod's house. *Mike* is sitting in a downstairs closet with the lights out, and Tod is doing his homework in the den, while watching TV. His mother stops at the door to the den and tells him to remember to turn off all the lights in the house before coming to bed. Tod waits a few moments after she has left, then says sharply, "*Mike*—out."

Using his ultrasonic eyes, *Mike* can see the closet door in the dark. He raises his metallic arm and opens the closet door.

Tod says, "*Mike*—here—shake."

Mike scans the den with his image-sensor camera. He locates Tod, approaches him, stops in front of him, and shakes his hand. In a deep, humanlike voice, he says, "Hi, Tod."

"Hi, *Mike*," Tod replies cheerfully. "*Mike*—lights—off."

Mike turns and goes to the nearest wall. He follows the wall (moving around objects he finds in his way) until he detects a light switch—with his ultrasonic and camera eyes. He knows which position of the switch is off, and which is on. This switch happens to be on. *Mike* turns it off. The room goes dark, lit only by the TV screen in the corner.

"Hey!" Tod yells. "Mistake—light—on."

"Sorry, Tod," *Mike* says, really sounding sincere. He turns the light back on, then leaves the den looking for other lights to turn off. He turns off all the lights in the other rooms and says loudly, "*Mike* is finished. Good job, *Mike*."

Tod calls, "*Mike*—home."

Mike returns to the den closet, enters it, spins around, and closes the door. In almost a whisper he says, "Good night, Tod. It is nine-fifteen."

Tod replies, "Good—night—*Mike*."

Mike searches his command table, finds "Good—night," and obeys the machine-language instructions stored with it: He waits fifteen seconds, then turns himself off.

HOLDEN AND *HERB*

Tod has written a book that describes how he has built (and is building) *Mike*.† Across America, people have written Tod and told him they are using his book and are building robots, too. One of those who used Tod's book as a starting point is Holden Caine, the inventor of *HERB*, another computer-controlled robot. Although *HERB* and *Mike*

† See Appendix A under "Robots."

have many functions in common, they are also quite different.

Holden recently took *HERB* on a visit to New York City. While in the city, *HERB* spent most of his time attracting crowds as a unique exhibit at the National Computer Conference.

HERB, like *Mike*, has a tiny microcomputer for a brain. Holden writes all of *HERB*'s programs on another computer and sends them along a wire, or *bus*, to *HERB*. The programs are sent along the bus to a *port*, or doorway, to *HERB*'s CPU brain.

HERB is a very independent robot. He has sensors to locate things around him. He checks the sensors thirty-two times a second, and, according to Holden, "he responds to any problems that occur, as soon as possible."

What kind of future does *HERB* have? Holden says *HERB* has plenty of room left on his chassis for new sensors and other hardware. Holden is currently adding ultrasonic sensors and is building *HERB* an arm. Holden sees *HERB* as a possible opponent for several of his favorite games. With his new arm and his electronic brain, *HERB* will be an active and formidable adversary in chess, backgammon, and other board games.

Holden Caine of Melville, New York, and his computerized robot *HERB*. *HERB* is about three feet tall, has a video camera for "eyes," and as he rolls about, he mumbles under his breath by making soft, musical tones.

How did Holden get interested in building a robot like *HERB?* According to Holden, "My interest in robots stems from an interest in computers. Robots represent one of the highest levels of computer application. There are very few projects that incorporate so many fascinating aspects such as mechanics, hardware, software, math, and *artificial intelligence.* The fact that no one has yet built a robot that can really be called intelligent makes a project such as my building *HERB* challenging."

BUILD YOUR OWN ROBOT

If you are like Robert, Tod, and Holden, and you build your own robot, you are a pioneer. Stick with it. It's possible you could build one of the most advanced home robots anywhere. To get started, pick up one of the books mentioned in Appendix A. Also, you might think about contacting groups like the U. S. Robotics Society, or the International Institute for Robotics—they can be great sources of information on robot parts, robot programs, and news about other robot inventors.‡ Also, why not share your project with a family member or a friend. You'll get your robot built faster, and you can both share the two hundred to five hundred dollars it's going to cost you to build it.

MEET THE *TURTLE*

What if you want to build a robot—but not from scratch? Then try a kit. There are kits advertised in home-computer and electronics magazines (see Appendix B). One of the most interesting little robots coming in kit form is the *Turtle* from Terrapin, Inc. A *Turtle* doesn't have any intelligence of its own (no *on-board* program), but it comes with an electric cord that can be hooked into the home computer. It's up to you to program the computer to act as the *Turtle*'s brain.

A *Turtle* can be taught to roam around your house, find its way through mazes, and search for an object with a certain shape—like a "*Turtle* house." A *Turtle* can also communicate: It can blink its two little LED "eyes," make beeping noises, and even write and draw squiggly pictures. And if you don't want to assemble *Turtle* yourself, you can buy it already assembled.

‡ For further information, contact General Secretary, Communications Center, U. S. Robotics Society, 616 University Avenue, Palo Alto, CA 94301; or contact Tom Carroll, U. S. Robotics Society, 7025 El Paseo, Long Beach, CA 90815. Contact T. D. Cowsert, Director, the International Institute for Robotics, P. O. Box 615, Pelaharchie, MS 39145. The two chief publishers of robot books are Hayden and TAB. See Appendices A, B, and C for additional information.

MAKE
YOUR
COMPUTER
TALK

Let's say you have a chemistry test tomorrow afternoon. You know that one of the big questions will be to name the elements in the Atomic Table—that's over a hundred names! Luckily, you have a home computer.

The first thing you do is grab your chemistry book and type all the elements' names into the computer's memory. Next, using a *flash-card* program you wrote for a history test, you have the computer print the names of the elements across the screen in large type. Each name sits on the screen for four seconds, then is replaced by the name of the next element. You stare intently at the screen. As the element name appears, your computer says the name and spells its symbol: "Hydrogen—H . . . Helium—H-e . . . Lithium—L-i . . ."

After running through the list almost a dozen times, you feel pretty confident. You feel ready for the second part of the flash-card program: a quiz on the elements' names. The computer's microphone is on the table next to the screen. You grab it and say, "Quiz."

The computer replies: "The quiz begins now. Element No. 1?"

You smile and answer, "Hydrogen—H."

"Correct," says the computer, flashing "Hydrogen (H)" on the screen. "Element No. 2?"

"Helium—H-e," you say.

"Correct," says the computer, flashing the second element's name and symbol. "Element No. 3?"

Oh no! You've forgotten element No. 3. You rack your brain for the answer. It won't come. After ten seconds the computer flashes the element's name and symbol on the screen, and says, "Lithium—L-i. Come on. Try harder."

Four seconds later the computer erases the screen and repeats, "Element No. 3?"

You could kick yourself for forgetting the element and for writing such a smug quiz program. "Lithium—L-i," you say.

"Correct," says the computer. "Element No. 4?"

SHOPPING FOR A
TALKING COMPUTER

Talking computers come in all shapes and sizes. There are the handheld games, like *Boris*, the talking chess computer. There are learning computers for children, like *Speak & Spell*, put out by Texas Instruments. And there are several wizard computers and super-game machines that come with *audio* (talking/listening) devices, or you can buy them as *add-ons*. One of these wizards, the Texas Instruments 99/4, comes with a canned vocabulary of 250 words—all stored in its huge ROM memory. Often they come as separate packages: *voice-recognition devices* to give your computer "ears," and *speech-synthesis devices* to enable your computer to talk.

EARS FOR YOUR COMPUTER

One of the best voice-recognition devices is *SpeechLab* by Heuristics. *SpeechLab* comes on a *circuit board* (or *card*) that you can plug into the computer. It has a large vocabulary, based on a command table stored in its memory.* Using the command table, you can have the computer do different things, depending on which command you give, using *Speech-Lab's* microphone. First you say the command, then the computer tries to match it with the commands in its table. If it finds a match, it obeys the command.

Can the computer always understand you no matter how you talk? No. How you talk is important. Even if you speak clearly and in your normal voice, *SpeechLab* (and other similar devices) can recognize you only nine times out of ten.

Can you walk up to the computer and say anything—including complete sentences? Again, no. This doesn't work for two reasons: First, a home computer has only a limited vocabulary—nowhere near the size of yours. Second, computers still do not have the ability to understand a *natural*, or spoken, language like English. They understand single English

---

* See the chapter titled "Paint a Picture."

commands (possibly consisting of several words), but not whole sentences at random.

AND NOW A FEW WORDS
FROM YOUR COMPUTER . . .

To get your computer to talk, you need a speech-synthesis device—a machine that can produce artificial speech from digital signals. Human speech is created both by *voiced sounds* and by *unvoiced sounds*. For example, when you say the word "fish," you create the unvoiced sound "f" by holding your vocal cords open and pushing air out of your vocal tract. (Try it.) You create the voiced sound "ish" by vibrating your vocal cords. The rate at which you vibrate them determines the *pitch* of your voice—more frequently, and your voice is high; less frequently, and it is deep. Speech, then, is the combination of unvoiced and voiced sounds that come from your mouth. These sounds are in the form of *pressure waves* that ripple through the air at a rate of 250 to 2,500 waves per second.†

One method of speech synthesis is to record a person's voice, store it in a computer's memory, and then reproduce it later. When the person says something—like "fish"—the sound wave can be divided into separate waves, or *parameters*, just as sunlight can be refracted through a prism to produce the various colors of the rainbow. A voice-recognition machine can take *slices*, or samples, of the original sound wave at a rate of up to 10,000 times a second (10 *kHz*).‡ Each time the machine records a sample, it divides it into its fundamental parameter waves. These waves are represented as voltages that pass through an analog-to-digital (A–D) converter and are transformed into on-off voltages, which are stored as a sequence of 1's and 0's in the computer's memory.*

The next step is to translate the digitized speech into actual sound—synthetic speech. First, the parameter waves (in the form of bytes) are sent to a D–A converter, which transforms the digital voltages into parameter voltages that resemble those formed originally when the person said the word "fish." Second, these voltages are sent through a speech synthesizer, which combines the separate parameter waves into a single synthetic sound wave. This wave—still in the form of electrical charges—is sent to a speaker, which produces the sound "fish."

---

† One wave per second is called one *"Hertz"* or *"Hz."* Thus 250 to 2,500 waves per second is 250 to 2,500 *Hertz* (or *Hz*).

‡ A thousand waves per second is a *"kiloHertz"* or *"kHz."* Thus 10,000 waves per second is 10 *kHz*.

* See the chapter titled "Paint a Picture."

One of the best speech-synthesis devices is the *CT-1 Speech Synthesizer* put out by Computalker Consultants. Like *SpeechLab,* the *CT-1* comes on a circuit board (or card), which you plug into your computer. The *CT-1* features two different methods to synthesize speech: a direct-parameter-control mode and a phonetic mode. *Direct parameter control* is similar to the method explained above. When you process your own voice through the *CT-1,* you will be surprised: Your computerized voice doesn't sound like it came from a science-fiction robot. Instead, you can recognize it—it sounds like you. On the other hand, there is something different about it—something eerie and machinelike. This comes from the *CT-1*'s valiant but not-quite-successful attempt to capture all the complex qualities of your voice.

The *CT-1* runs on a home computer, and its speed and memory are still quite limited. This prevents it from taking sufficient samples of a voice, and from dividing those samples up into an adequate number of parameter waves. But it still does a good job, all things considered. And if you are disappointed that you don't sound like a robot from some Hollywood movie, you can order *CT-1* to produce a robot voice instead.

You can also have *CT-1* use another method to synthesize human speech: the *phonetic mode.* In this mode, you use "sounds like" spellings of words, or *phonemes,* to produce speech. For example, you can type in "HHEHLOW," and your computer says, "Hello." The word contains the following phonemes: "HH," "EH," "L," and "OW." The computer stores the phonemes as 1's and o's in its memory; then, on your command, it sends them to the synthesizer and speaker, which convert them into the spoken word "Hello."

PLAY AN
ORCHESTRA

How does a home computer make music? First, you write a *music program*. When your music program runs through the computer, it generates voltages that are sent through the computer's *music-synthesis chip*, translated into voltages analogous to sound waves, then converted into actual sound when they are sent to a speaker and cause the *cones* to vibrate and force ripples through the air. You hear the music when the sound waves in the air rush into your ear and begin vibrating your eardrum, or *tympanum*.

The quality of the tones that come out of the speaker depends in large part on the *speed* and *storage capacity* of the computer. Even a small computer can reproduce a single note, or *pitch*, of music. But most music is more varied, more complex. For example, why isn't an A note sung by an opera singer the same as an A note played on a trumpet? The difference is *timbre*, or musical color. Timbre comes from undertones in a musical sound wave. These are the subordinate frequencies that often are multiples of the basic frequency (the A note). You don't hear the undertones as separate pitches, but as an enrichment or shading of the original tone.

Large computers used by recording companies are able to capture and reproduce all the characteristics of a sound wave, including timbre. They can accurately reproduce a middle C on a piano, a chord strummed on a guitar, or a three-part harmony sung by a vocal group. This is because they operate in billionths of a second and can store millions of pieces (or bits) of information in main memory. Since home computers cannot do this, they must instead try to capture samples, or slices, of the sound waves, store and digitize these, then reproduce them. The resulting tones, or sounds, are not as full and rich as those produced in professional studios, but they are definitely music. And, as home computers get faster and can store more information, their music improves.

HOW THE WIZARDS MAKE MUSIC

Most of the new wizard computers come with a music-synthesis chip (or circuit card), or you can buy one as an add-on. Either way, you get the chance to compose your own music or play the computer like an organ. (Usually you use the regular typewriterlike keyboard that comes with the computer. However, more and more computers are being sold with piano and organ keyboard attachments.)

But what if you can't play music, and you don't know a note from a measure? Then be sure to pick up a program like *Music Teacher* from VideoBrain. *Music Teacher* gives you the basics of how to read music even as you are learning to play.

After you have gotten the basics under control, why not try to make some of your own music? To show how easy it is to get started, let's take a look at how you make music on the Texas Instruments 99/4 computer. The *TI-99/4* has an expanded version of *BASIC*, which includes sound commands that activate the synthesizer chip. To make music on the *TI-99/4*, the most important command you need to know is "CALL SOUND." With just that one command, you can produce tones of different pitch, volume, and duration. The basic form of the sound command is "CALL SOUND(D,P,V)." The "D" is for the *duration*, or time, of the tone. It is measured in terms of *milliseconds* (thousandths of a second).

The "P" stands for the *pitch*, or frequency, of the sound. A high pitch means a high note or tone. A low pitch means a low note. Pitch is measured in Hertz, the number of sound waves, or cycles, per second. The *TI-99/4* computer can produce sounds with a pitch from 110 Hertz (below low C on the piano) to more than 16kHz (*kiloHertz*—more than 16,000 sound waves per second). This is impressive, since any sound with a frequency (or pitch) higher than 16,000 cycles per second is beyond the limit of human hearing.

"V" is the last part of the command. It stands for *volume*. You can adjust the volume of your music from "0" to "30," with "0" (or "1," which here is the same) producing the loudest sound, and "30" producing the softest.

Now that you are familiar with the "CALL SOUND" command, let's give it a try. For example, if you typed

CALL SOUND(1000,262,2)

The pipe organ has been called the "original synthetic instrument," since it was the first musical instrument to *synthesize,* or imitate, other instruments by using its pipes to produce the *timbre* (or musical undertones) characteristic of those instruments. Students and professors in the Soloworks Lab at the University of Pittsburgh have built an organ that is controlled by two home computers (an *Altair 8800b* and an *Intellec 8/MOD 80*). Using the *MUSIC* language, a student can compose a song on the graphics terminal (left), then have the organ play it, imitating, say, the viola and flute sections in an orchestra. [Reprinted with permission from *The BYTE Book of Computer Music,* copyright © 1978, BYTE Publications, Inc., McGraw-Hill, Inc., all rights reserved.]

Steve Roberts of Louisville, Kentucky, built a musical instrument out of a *Z-2D* home computer made by Cromemco; a sixty-one-note organ keyboard from Kimball Organ Company; a typewriter keyboard; a couple of picture screens; and miscellaneous other computer and electronic equipment. Steve can make music by typing commands on his typewriter keyboard, or he can "play" his computer directly from the organ keyboard. According to Steve, this is "*polyphony*" (multiple-note chords) "made easy."

you would get a middle C (on the piano). The sound—the musical note—would last 1,000 milliseconds, or 1 second. It would have a frequency of 262 cycles per second (262 Hertz), which is equal to middle C. It would have a loudness of "2," which is very loud.

Using the "SOUND" command, you could write a program to play the notes on the *scale* from middle C to high C:

```
10 CALL SOUND(1000,262,2)
20 CALL SOUND(1000,294,2)
30 CALL SOUND(1000,330,2)
40 CALL SOUND(1000,349,2)
50 CALL SOUND(1000,392,2)
```

```
60 CALL SOUND(1000,440,2)
70 CALL SOUND(1000,494,2)
80 CALL SOUND(1000,523,2)
90 END
```

This program plays one *octave*, or eight notes, from middle C to high C: "C," "D," "E," "F," "G," "A," "B," and high "C." Using just these notes, you could program a song—either one of your own, or one you already know.

On the other hand, most songs require more than simple notes; they require *chords*, several notes played at the same time. The *TI-99/4* is capable of chords with up to three notes. For example, to program the chord "C-E-G," you would type

CALL SOUND(1000,262,2,330,15,392,2)

The computer would play the chord, accentuating the "C" (262 Hz) and "G" (392 Hz) with a volume of "2," and playing the "E" (330 Hz) more softly with a volume of "15."

Now, to demonstrate that you can program a real song (albeit a simple one), let's take that all-time favorite, "Happy Birthday," and program it on the *TI-99/4* computer. The musical *score* for "Happy Birthday" looks like this:

HAPPY BIRTHDAY

Programming the song is easy. Since the music says the song's *tempo*, or pace, is "*allegro*"—or happy, cheerful, and lively—let's give the notes in the song the following duration:

Eighth note (♪)	. . .	250 "milliseconds" (a quarter second)
Quarter note (♩)	. . .	500 "milliseconds" (a half second)
Half note (♩)	. . .	1,000 "milliseconds" (a full second)

The only other thing you need to decide is the song's *dynamics*—its loudness (the height, or *amplitude*, of the sound wave). This song is usually played and sung at birthday parties, which are pretty noisy. Let's choose "4" for *forte*, or loud.

Also, related to the song's dynamics is the *accent* placed on certain *beats* (or notes) in each *measure*. Since "Happy Birthday" is *triple meter*, or three beats to the measure (¾), the basic pattern is an accented beat followed by two unaccented beats. We'll leave the unaccented beats at forte ("4"), and make the accented beat *fortissimo* ("2"), or very loud.

To make the program more readable, let's use "REM," the *comment* command. Whenever a line begins with "REM," the computer knows that what follows is a message for people, not a command for it to process.

Next, you take the notes in the last eight *bars* of the song and just plug in the pitch and duration values, and you get a program that plays "Happy Birthday":

HAPPY BIRTHDAY
(Played by the *TI-99/4* Computer)

```
1 REM    Song: "Happy Birthday"
2 REM    Meter: Three-four Time
3 REM    Key: F
4 REM
5 REM
6 REM    Define Notes (Pitches) Used in Song
7 REM
10 LET  C=262
20 LET  D=294
30 LET  E=330
40 LET  F=349
50 LET  G=392
60 LET  A=440
70 LET  BFLAT=466
80 LET  HIC=523
90 LET  HID=587
100 LET  HIE=659
105 REM
106 REM      Define Dynamics (Loudness) of Song
107 REM
110 LET  FORTE=4
115 LET  ACCENT=2
116 REM
117 REM      Define Tempo (Pace or Speed) of Song
```

```
118 REM
120 LET EIGHTH=250
130 LET QUARTER=500
140 LET HALF=1000
145 REM
146 REM        Begin Playing "Happy Birthday"
147 REM
148 REM        *** First Measure
149 REM
150 GOSUB  1000'    Two Eighth-note Middle C's
155 REM
156 REM        *** Second Measure
157 REM
160 CALL SOUND(QUARTER,D,ACCENT)
170 CALL SOUND(QUARTER,C,FORTE)
180 CALL SOUND(QUARTER,F,FORTE)
185 REM
186 REM        *** Third Measure
187 REM
190 CALL SOUND(HALF,E,ACCENT)
200 GOSUB  1000'    Two Eighth-note Middle C's
205 REM
206 REM        *** Fourth Measure
207 REM
210 CALL SOUND(QUARTER,D,ACCENT)
220 CALL SOUND(QUARTER,C,FORTE)
230 CALL SOUND(QUARTER,G,FORTE)
235 REM
236 REM        ***Fifth Measure
237 REM
240 CALL SOUND(HALF,F,ACCENT)
250 GOSUB  1000'    Two Eighth-note Middle C's
255 REM
256 REM        *** Sixth Measure
257 REM
260 CALL SOUND(QUARTER,HIC,ACCENT)
270 CALL SOUND(QUARTER,A,FORTE)
280 CALL SOUND(QUARTER,F,FORTE)
285 REM
286 REM        *** Seventh Measure
287 REM
290 CALL SOUND(QUARTER,E,ACCENT)
300 CALL SOUND(QUARTER,D,FORTE)
```

```
310 CALL SOUND(EIGHTH,BFLAT,FORTE)
320 CALL SOUND(EIGHTH,BFLAT,FORTE)
325 REM
326 REM        *** Eighth Measure
327 REM
330 CALL SOUND(QUARTER,A,ACCENT)
340 CALL SOUND(QUARTER,F,FORTE)
350 CALL SOUND(QUARTER,G,FORTE)
355 REM
356 REM        *** Ninth (and Final) Measure
357 REM
360 CALL SOUND(HALF,F,ACCENT)
370 END
1000 REM
1010 REM        *** Two Eighth-note Middle C's
1020 REM
1030 CALL SOUND(EIGHTH,C,FORTE)
1040 CALL SOUND(EIGHTH,C,FORTE)
1050 RETURN
```

THE MUSIC MACHINE

Our example—"Happy Birthday"—was simple, but your music needn't be. After you get the hang of programming songs on your computer, you can move on to Beethoven, Mozart, Scott Joplin, Earl Scruggs, Steve Wonder, and the BeeGees. And as your music grows, so should your system. Several companies, including Proteus Computing and ALF Products, Inc., offer advanced *music synthesizers*, which you can hook up to a home computer.

The ALF *Music Synthesizer* offers a wide range of features for the budding computer musician. The *Synthesizer* produces pitches using a crystal-controlled circuit that never needs tuning. There are so many pitches available, you can create notes that cover the full eight octaves of a piano and even fall between piano keys. For example, on a piano you play an "E," then an "F." On the *Synthesizer*, you can play an "E," then three notes, then an "F."

The *Synthesizer* lets you choose among 256 different volume levels (dynamics). You can program it to play a lullaby for a baby or a fight song for a school football team.

If you and your friends buy synthesizers together, you can combine up to three synthesizers and produce musical chords of up to nine tones at a time. Then to get the best music possible, you can plug all three syn-

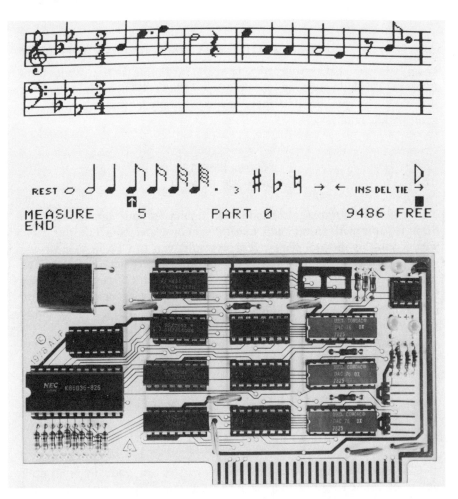

You can turn your home computer into an electronic musician by plugging in a *music synthesizer* board. Once your board is installed, you can compose music, play it, and edit it. [Courtesy of ALF Products, Inc.]

thesizers into your amplifier and stereo speakers and program real stereo sound.

The *Synthesizer* comes with a *music entry language,* which lets you program your songs using the computer's game paddles. Using the left paddle, you can select from a song menu, which includes the type of note you want (quarter note, half note, etc.), and whether you want a sharp, a flat, a rest, and so on. By moving the stick on the right paddle, you can move a tiny round cursor across a *musical staff* on the picture screen to the place on the staff where you want a note placed. Then you push the button on the paddle, and the note appears on the staff.

In addition, there are several commands you can use simply for music entry and editing. For example, by typing "MEASURE:23" on the keyboard, you can display your song, or score, beginning at the twenty-third measure. To play your song, you just type "PLAY." Then while the song is playing, you can vary its *tempo*, or speed, simply by rotating one of the game-paddle knobs.

SOUND EFFECTS
FOR YOUR GAMES

A musical computer can add new drama to your games. You can begin a game with music, add musical sections, and conclude the game with a song or musical phrase. For example, you can begin a space-war game with the theme song from your favorite science-fiction movie. You can start your detective game with the song from a TV cops-and-robbers show. You can begin a football game with a fight song or cheer. Or you can start the action in a haunted-castle game with weird, spooky music that sends icicle shivers down your back.

And you're not limited to music, either. Some wizards and sound synthesizers also let you make up your own *noises*. For example, on the TI-99/4 you can produce a noise just by making the pitch in the "CALL SOUND" command into a *negative*, or minus, number. One command will give you up to four seconds of nice loud noise:

CALL SOUND(4500,-20,1)

By experimenting with noises and tones, you can gradually build up a *library* of canned sounds to plug into your games. You can add creaky-door sounds, gunshots, laser blasts, screeches, and shrieks. You can program growls, roars, explosions, whistles, and snores. You can dream up bells, creepy groans, bawling engines, hiccups, and sneezes. All these sound effects will make your games exciting and realistic.

PAINT
A PICTURE

C arol is a computer artist. Using an electric *light pen* to "sketch" pictures on the screen, Carol composes a scene of herself horseback riding. By typing certain keys on the computer, she is able to transform her sketch into a detailed picture.

How does the computer do it? It takes the figures and scene in Carol's sketch and replaces them with artistic images Carol has stored in the computer's memory. How did these images get into the computer's memory? First, Carol took pictures of some of her favorite subjects, including mountains, dogs, horses, herself, her family, some of her friends, and the ocean. Next, she entered copies of these photos into the computer by tracing their outlines on a *digitizer*. The digitizer translates Carol's picture outlines into picture elements (pixels), or locations on the screen. The pixels are stored in the computer's memory as a sequence of bytes (of eight bits—1's and 0's). When Carol has entered a whole picture, she stores it in a computer *file* with a designation like CAROL, MOUNTAIN, HORSE, etc. These files are the master images for Carol's pictures. After she does a drawing of her own, she tells the computer which master images she wants to appear in the drawing. The computer consults a *table of master images* that it has stored in memory. It retrieves the images Carol requests—like HORSE, FENCE, and CAROL—and rotates and positions them to fit the scene Carol has drawn. It builds a complete picture from the separate images, then "paints" the picture on the screen. Underneath the picture it asks, "How's this?"

If Carol isn't satisfied, she tells the computer to make some changes —*rotate* a figure fifteen degrees, raise an arm, darken the green in the pine tree. The computer makes the changes, and seconds later it has a new picture. Again it asks, "How's this?"

Carol likes what she sees. She types, "Perfect."

"Title? File name?" asks the computer.

"The Grand Leap. LEAP," types Carol.

When the computer gets the painting's title, it does two things: First, it prints the title under the painting in big block letters. Second, it stores the painting in a disk file named "LEAP."

BOXED IN

If you are interested in making pictures, try a home computer. The newest home computers can produce pictures with up to 256 different colors and up to 8 levels of brightness. What is more, the pictures are smooth and realistic, since they are made of as many as a quarter-million pixels!

Before you work up to pictures like Carol's, you need to learn how to produce the basic elements—points, lines, curves, shaded areas, etc.—that you combine to create more complicated pictures. To demonstrate how to produce a box, for example, let's use one of the "wizard" computers—the *Atari 400*.

GRAPHICS KEYBOARD

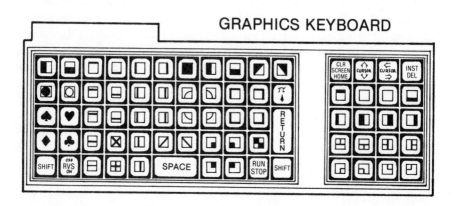

The *Atari 400* and *800* computers use *BASIC* as their main programming language: *Atari BASIC* has been expanded to include *graphics* (picture-making) *commands* along with the standard *BASIC* commands (like "GOTO," "FOR . . . NEXT," etc.). There are five graphics commands that are useful any time you want to make computer art: "GRAPHICS," "COLOR," "SETCOLOR," "PLOT," and "DRAWTO."

The first command, "GRAPHICS A," separates the screen into *graphics* (your picture) and *text* (your labels and messages). It also defines how many pixels the screen is divided into, depending on the value of "A."

The second command, "COLOR," sets one of the four color *registers* (memory locations) so that you can see what you're drawing on the screen.

The third command, "SETCOLOR X,Y," allows you to choose the colors for your picture. "Y" is the number of the color you have chosen.

"X" lets you choose what part of the screen you want to color. When you are drawing pictures with different colors (and setting "Y" to different numbers), you set "X" to "O." When you want to change the color in the *text window* (where you have your labels and messages), you set "X" to "2." Finally, when you want the screen background to change color, you set "X" to "4."

The fourth command, "PLOT C,R," lets you color one pixel—the one at column "C" and row "R." The size of the pixel (whether it looks like a block or a small dot) depends on which "GRAPHICS" mode you have chosen. For example, if you write a program starting with the command "GRAPHICS 3," you have told the Atari computer to divide the screen into 39 columns and 20 rows of pixels, leaving 4 lines at the bottom for labels and messages. Multiplying 39 by 20 gives you 780 pixels on the screen. This is *low resolution* and results in blocky pictures, but it is just what you need for a picture of boxes.

The fifth command, "DRAWTO," enables you to draw lines when it is used along with "PLOT." For example, if you typed this little program into the computer:

```
10 GRAPHICS 3
20 COLOR 1
30 SETCOLOR 0,3
40 PLOT 0,5
50 DRAWTO 38,5
60 END
```

then typed "RUN" (and pushed the "ENTER" key), the computer would draw a flat, straight, red line all the way across the screen. The line would begin at the pixel located at column 0 and row 5 ("PLOT 0,5"), and end at the pixel at column 38 and (still) row 5 ("DRAWTO 38,5").

Now you are ready to draw boxes—boxes that move and change colors. You already know how to change colors—you change the value of "Y" in the "SETCOLOR X,Y" command. Moving pictures are just as easy: You just change the value of "A" in the "GRAPHICS A" command. You can try this out with the following program:

```
10 COLOR 1
20 FOR R=0 TO 15
30 SETCOLOR 0,R
40 C=160: R=96
50 FOR A=7 TO 3 STEP −2
60 GRAPHICS A
70 C=C/2: R=R/2: PLOT C,R
80 PLOT C−2,R−2: DRAWTO C+2,R−2
90 DRAWTO C+2,R+2: DRAWTO C−2,R+2
100 DRAWTO C−2,R−2
110 PLOT C−4,R−4: DRAWTO C+4,R−4
120 DRAWTO C+4,R+4: DRAWTO C−4,R+4
130 DRAWTO C−4,R−4
140 NEXT A
150 NEXT R
160 END
```

This program creates three boxes that grow and change colors. You start feeling dizzy if you watch the boxes too long. In fact, they're almost hypnotic.

If you look at this program closely, you will see it is really pretty simple. In fact, it is much shorter than the "TRAPPED!" program in the chapter titled "You're Trapped!" But there are two new twists you haven't seen until now: First, there is a *nested loop* in this program—that's one loop inside another loop. The way the two loops work is very similar to the way the big (minutes) hand and the small (hours) hand on a clock work. On a clock, the minutes hand has to go around twelve numbers before the hours hand moves one number. In the program above, the *inside loop* (which changes the size of the boxes) has to go around three times (where A="7," "5," and "3") before the *outside loop* (which changes the color) goes around once. Second, the inside loop counts *backward*—by two. By including "STEP −2" in the "FOR" command, you get the loop counter ("A") to start at "7" (for "GRAPHICS 7"), then go to "5" (for "GRAPHICS 5"), and end up at "3" (for "GRAPHICS 3").

BEYOND BOXES

Boxes that move and change color are nice, but they are a long way from the kind of pictures Carol was painting. On the other hand, they have introduced you to pictures made by combining *geometric shapes*, a type of art that computers do particularly well. One person who has become quite good at getting the computer to make pictures of this sort is Joe Jacobson of Maple Shade, New Jersey.

Over the years, Joe and his friends have made and collected over a hundred computer art pictures like the one on p. 76. Joe has created his art using various devices, including a programmable calculator, a *Tektronix 4051 intelligent terminal* (very much like a home computer), and various electronic and mechanical *plotters*.

Geometric patterns, according to Joe, can be created in the following way. *First,* you sit down and sketch a pattern you think would be particularly beautiful. *Second,* you have to come up with an *algorithm,* or set of steps, that the computer follows to compute the points in the pattern, then have the plotter draw them. This algorithm can be as simple as a list of points which the computer just repeats as commands to the plotter, or as complicated as a long mathematical formula. *Third,* you translate the algorithm into an actual program (written in *BASIC, APL, PASCAL,* etc.). *Fourth and last,* you run the program and operate the plotter—you

Joe Jacobson creates his intricate and beautiful pictures using an "intelligent" graphics terminal (a *Tektronix 4051*)—really a home computer in disguise. Creating "geometric" art on a home computer is a great way to sharpen your math skills. You use math to build *models* of the real world—anything from the dollars in your allowance to the flight path of a rocket ship. Even the most complicated math formulas make more sense when they are drawn graphically—as pictures—on your computer screen! [Courtesy of Joe Jacobson and *Creative Computing* magazine.]

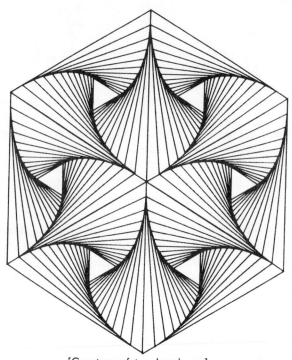

[Courtesy of Joe Jacobson.]

may, for example, need to insert different colored pens into the plotter's mechanical arm to get it to draw a multicolored geometric pattern.

The more skilled you become at making geometric patterns, the more elaborate and complex the patterns can become. Working with some of the "wizard" computers, you can create 3-D (three-dimensional) patterns that you can rotate, magnify, shrink, and set in motion.

If you become really good at producing graceful and unusual geometric shapes using your computer, you might do as Joe Jacobson does and exhibit your artwork at school, or at one of the various computer or science-fiction conventions that are held throughout the country.

WRITE A
POEM

Here is a poem my computer made up:

> The stuffy balloons
> giggled,
> The ice cream motorcycles
> wiggled,
> As the men in the town
> With the girls all around,
> Jumped over a giant red
> pickle.

Pretty bad, right? That figures: I'm not a good poet, and what poetry the computer knows, it learned from me.

Computer poetry may not always be pretty, but it is fun. How can you turn your computer into a poet? If you like *free-verse poetry* (poetry without *rhyme* or *meter*), it's pretty simple. You just sit down and think up all the words you would like to see in the poems. Then you feed them to the computer in the form of a *table*, or list.

You don't want the computer just to read from the list. You could do that yourself, and it would be boring. You want your computer to act like a poet, to be creative. To do this, you add the element of chance by writing a program that includes commands like "RND" and "RAN-DOMIZE."* This way, the computer will choose words at random from its word table. Next, type "RUN," and get ready for something bizarre

---

* See the chapter titled "You're Trapped!"

and unexpected. Something like:

> I you the trucks
>   was
>   smiling trees
> into
>   mad comic book kittens
> will be were happy
>   bicycle treats

If this is a little too far out, you need to teach your computer poet a few more things about poems (and about English!). The way you do this is to set up a basic structure of a poem—a *skeleton*—which includes where the subjects and predicates of sentences go; where you want the nouns, verbs, adverbs, and prepositions. You decide on *punctuation*—commas, periods, capitalization, and so on. Then you give the computer a *vocabulary*: In its memory you store lists of funny or beautiful nouns, silly adverbs, melodic adjectives, active verbs, etc. If you want your computer's poetry to rhyme, you build *rhyming tables*: lists of all the rhyming words in the computer's vocabulary. And if you really want to get fancy, you add *meter*, or rhythm, for all the words.†

When the program actually runs, it will refer to your poem skeleton. If it needs a noun, it fetches a noun from the *noun table*, puts it into the empty noun slot on the line, then looks at the next part of the sentence. If that's a verb, the computer gets a verb from the *verb table* and adds that to the line. The computer makes sure when it picks out each word that its meter value is correct. If not, the computer rejects that word and tries a new one. After the computer has completed a pair of lines that are supposed to rhyme, it checks to make sure if the last words in each line actually rhyme—that they come from the same table of rhyming words. If not, the computer searches the table for words that rhyme, and substitutes them for the nonrhyming words. When it has finished building an entire poem from the original poem skeleton, the computer prints the complete poem on the screen, or—if you have a talking computer poet— it recites the poem to you and asks if you like it.

But what if you think the poem is awful? Just tell the computer. You can afford to be picky: The computer isn't sensitive about its poetry. It

---

† *Meter* is usually measured in terms of: (1) the number of *beats*, or accented syllables, per line; or (2) small groups of accented and unaccented syllables called *feet*. Each *foot* has a special name. For example, a group of two syllables— one accented, the other unaccented—is called an *iamb*, or *iambic foot*. You build a line in your poem by stringing the feet together.

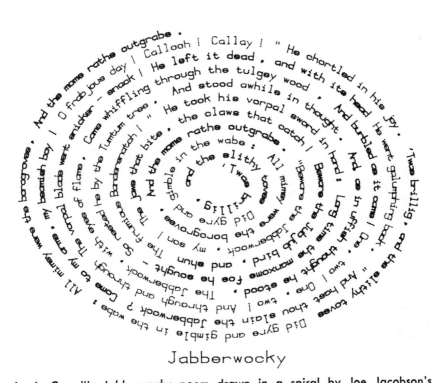

Jabberwocky

Lewis Carroll's *Jabberwocky* poem drawn in a spiral by Joe Jacobson's computer. [Picture by Joe Jacobson. (From a program written by Michael Grossman.)]

will just go back and build a new poem. And since it can produce a poem every couple of seconds, in only a few minutes you can have dozens of original computer poems. In fact,

> It will surprise you,
> Like it surprised me,
> How quickly you will be
> Swimming in a paper sea
> Of computer poetry.

MAKE
A POSTER

On the morning of July 21, 1969, English-language newspapers around the world carried the big, bold headline:

MAN ON MOON

The day before, American astronauts had touched down on the surface of the moon; and astronaut Neil Armstrong had taken his "giant leap for mankind." The headlines were in large, *banner* print befitting the occasion.

Banner signs that look like newspaper headlines are great to use in your bedroom or rec room, or to herald a special event, like the opening of a school play, or an upcoming Heart Fund bikeathon. How do you make a banner sign using a home computer? There are several ways: *First,* you can use a *computer plotter* to draw the letters in the banner with a pen or pencil held in a mechanical arm. *Second,* you can use a *graphics printer* to print the banner using special graphics characters. *Third,* you can use an *alphanumeric printer* that produces the graphics characters by overstriking its numbers, letters, and punctuation marks. (*Overstriking* is when you print more than one character in a single space. For example, you can create a ⊠, a boxlike graphics character, by overstriking a "T," "X," "H," and an "L"; or you can make a ⊠, by overstriking a "O," "+," and an "X.")

Another way to create a banner is to build large-scale letters from regular alphanumeric letters. For example, you can use the "PRINT" statement from *BASIC* to print a giant, banner-sized letter "A" out of normal-sized letter "A's." Your "A" program would look like this:

10 PRINT"   A"

20 PRINT"   AAA"

30 PRINT"   AA AA"

40 PRINT"   AA   AA"

50 PRINT"   AAAAAAAAA"

60 PRINT"   AA   AA"

70 PRINT" AA   AA"

80 PRINT"AA   AA"

90 END

If you don't feel like typing in giant letters every time you make a banner, you can create a *table of letters*, which you can attach to all of your banner programs. Then all you have to do is type the word you want printed out as a banner, and the program will search the table, pull out the right giant letters, and print them on the screen or printer.

There are many good banner programs listed in computer-hobby magazines.* Some of the programs produce particularly nice banners by

* See Appendix B for a list of the major magazines.

using a *character-matrix* to print individual letters. A five-by-five character-matrix, for example, is a rectangle broken into five rows and five columns of *little* rectangles, or *cells*. Each letter uses one character-matrix. Different cells are blocked out by overstriking—or by using graphics characters—depending on which letter is being printed. For example, the letter "A" printed on an eighteen-by-twenty-one-character-matrix would look like this:

This matrix letter "A" was produced on an alphanumeric computer printer. Thanks to Rick Langston for doing the programming. Thanks to Stan Gilliam for drawing the matrix.

Some of the banner programs let you print the large letters either horizontally or vertically, of regular or double width, and even allow you to create new letters, numbers, or other characters. Using this feature you can invent a whole new alphabet.

JOIN
A GAME
NETWORK

Having a home computer is great, but do you know how to make it even better? Tie your computer in with your friends' computers. How? Over the phone.

Once you have hooked the computer up to the phone, it can talk with other home computers, with store computers, bank computers, government computers, and computers at the offices where your mom and dad work. How do computers talk on the phone? They use a *modem* (MOdulator/DEModulator). The telephone plugs into the modem, and the modem is plugged into the computer.

The modem translates your computer's *digital* signal into two *tones* (for a "1" bit and a "0" bit of information). The tones are similar to those stored on a tape recorder. They are amplified, then sent into the telephone's mouthpiece, and are transmitted over the phone line to the other computer. When the other computer answers, it sends tones back over the phone line. They emerge from the line via the phone earpiece, are picked up by a microphone in the modem, then converted into digital signals and sent to the computer. The bits are sent one at a time, grouped into packages of eight bits—a byte.

To enable the computer to make telephone calls, you'll also need an *interface board*, or *card*, which acts like a bus depot, where incoming and outgoing data are routed, waiting to be transmitted or stored in the computer.

Further, make sure you choose a standard connection among the computer, the interface card, and the modem. This way a standard signal —based on *signal duration, current,* and *voltage*—can be sent from the computer to the interface card and on to the modem. The connection

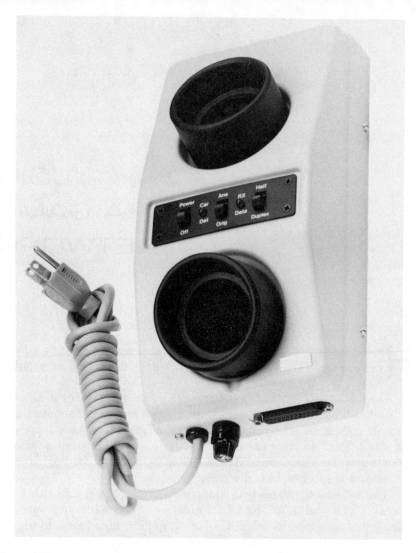

The modem or *acoustic coupler* transforms a home computer's electrical pulses into audible tones (sounds) that can be transmitted over a regular phone line. When a home computer "receives" a call from another home computer, its modem converts the tones back into electrical pulses to be processed inside the computer. [Courtesy of Datec, Inc.]

used most frequently is the *RS-232C*, developed by the Electronics Industries Association (EIA). RS-232C cords come with standard plugs and sockets that fit into the computer and the modem.

If your computer is on the phone so much, won't it hog the line and not let anyone else make calls? Not likely. The reason is that the computer and its friends will be "talking" at a rate of 1,200 *baud*—1,200 Bits of AUdio Data—per second. Those are 120 bytes a second—or 120 *characters*. It is equivalent to a full, double-spaced page of information every 16 seconds. At that rate, most conversations will last less than a minute.

Also, it is likely that the phone company will install new computer telephone lines when the computer traffic increases. These lines will be of a higher *band width* and permit computers to talk much faster—probably at a rate of 9,600 baud. That's a page of information every two seconds! Also, the computer will probably use the phone at night while you are asleep. That's the time when human traffic and long-distance rates are at their lowest.

So your family computer can make phone calls. What good does that do you? For starters, you can call up a friend and work on homework problems together, using the two computers to do the calculating and the communicating. You can also play games on the phone: games with you vs. your friend, your computer vs. your friend's computer, or all of you vs. each other. Or you might show your computer to your deaf friends. Hooking a computer to a deaf person's telephone would enable him to make phone calls: He types what he wants to say on his computer, his computer sends the message to someone else's computer, and that computer displays the message on the screen or prints it on a *TTY* (Tele-TYpewriter). It would be a revolution in the lives of two deaf friends if they had a way to "talk" to each other on the phone.

Another idea: You can dial up a computer department store—*The Source*—in McLean, Virginia, and get the store's computer to send your computer new programs or data. Or why not start a program exchange yourself? You could set it up among your friends and relatives—those who are local and those who are out of town.

Big government and business computers all over the world are linked together in *networks*. Now, for the first time, there is a network of home computers: *PCNET*, set up by the People's Computer Company (PCC), a nonprofit educational group in Menlo Park, California. The only things you need to get on the network are: (1) a standard home computer; (2) a modem; and (3) *PAN*, the network's programming language.*

Why join a network of home computers? When you first get a home computer, you will be busy writing your own games, graphics programs, homework and music programs, puzzles, quizzes, and mazes. Why not join a network and share these programs with others in return for some interesting programs they've written? You could type up a *catalog* that listed the names of all of your special programs, what each does, what language it is in, etc. Suggest to your friends and relatives that they do the same. Then you could exchange catalogs, decide on what programs you would like to get, and have your computer place a late-night call to the other computers to get the programs you selected.

What else can you do on a network? You can send your friends *electronic mail* over a home-computer network. You can also maintain a lively

---

* People's Computer Company (PCC) publishes information about *PCNET* in its two magazines, *Recreational Computing* and *Dr. Dobb's Journal*. See Appendix B.

electronic bulletin board. You and your friends can exchange programs, games, the latest news, good jokes—messages of all kinds. You have your computer make late-night phone calls to the other computers and store the program or message in those computers' bulletin-board *files*. The next day, to see what messages were on your bulletin board, you would simply turn on the computer and have it print out the bulletin-board file on the picture screen or typewriter.

DESIGN A
SECRET
CODE

With the advent of *electronic mail* and *electronic money*, your home computer will be tied into your family's telephone, TV, and radio. Many of your family's records will be available to friends, relatives, teachers, banks, and government agencies—over the phone line. When this happens, you'll see a new kind of criminal appear on the scene: *the information burglar.* He won't enter your home by any of the traditional means—by picking a lock or by forcing open a window. Instead, he'll make a simple phone call: His computer will telephone your computer, then drain it dry of all your family's private records and information. Like burglars in the past, he'll work at night, stealthily and noiselessly, while your family is asleep. Within seconds he'll be done. He'll know everything about you, and you won't be any wiser.

Is there anything you can do to protect your information? Fortunately, there is. It's called *cryptography*, the science of encrypting, or transforming, information into nonsense to anyone who is not meant to have access to it.

Already there are canned programs you can buy that will put a cryptographic *lock* on your home computer. Or you can develop your own lock. To protect your family's information, you need a *cipher*. A cipher is a precise list of steps—a formula or algorithm—that you follow to transform or *encode* your data. After you develop a cipher that you like, you convert it into computer commands—a program that runs on your computer and activates the cipher.

All of your family's private, important, or sensitive information can be transformed by the cipher program into secret code. But how do you use the information if it's coded? Is there any way to get it back? There is.

You need to write a second program, a *cryptanalyst*, which transforms, or *decodes*, the information back into normal, readable form.

How do you make a cipher? Making a complicated, almost foolproof cipher will require you to do some hard thinking and some more reading.* On the other hand, developing a simple cipher is easy. Transforming and encoding information comes naturally to computers: That's how they operate. They are electronic devices that regulate and switch voltages along tiny circuits. To make computers process and store information, a low (or zero) voltage is coded as a "o," and a high voltage as a "1." The 1's and o's become information when they are grouped together—eight at a time—into *bytes*. The bytes are coded in two different ways: There are binary bytes, which store numbers used in arithmetic; and there are *ASCII* bytes for storing everything else.†

To show how a simple cipher might be created, let's say you have a letter to a close friend named Mary stored on the computer, and you don't want anyone else to see it. Say the letter starts with a traditional "Dear Mary." Stored as ASCII bytes, these first two words look like this:

```
01000100  01100101  01100001  01110010
01001101  01100001  01110010  01111001
```

Your cipher would have only one step:

Take each bit (a "1" or a "o") in the byte. If the bit is a 1, change it to a o. If it is a o, change it to a 1.

Next you would convert the cipher into a computer program, run the letter through it, and the letter would be *encrypted*—protected so no one but you would know its real contents. After running through the cipher program, "Dear Mary" would look like this:

```
10111011  10011010  10011110  10001101
10110010  10011110  10001101  10000110
```

If you tried to print these new, encrypted bytes on a terminal or printer, they might print as meaningless characters.‡ To anyone scanning your "Dear Mary" letter file, it would look like machine-language code, or stray bits and bytes—*garbage*. They wouldn't waste a second look.

---

* See recent issues of computer magazines. Also, visit the library and look under headings like "cipher," "codes," and "cryptography."

† See the ASCII Coding Chart in Appendix E, and the list of decimal and binary Numbers in Appendix F.

‡ If your home computer is like most computers and ignores the *high-order*, or leftmost, bit in each byte, then you will get some stray characters (like "," "\," "," and ">"), some letters, and some numbers.

But what if you want to see the letter again? Then you'll need a crypt-analyst program. In this case it's the same as the cipher program. When you run the encrypted letter through the cipher program a second time, it restores it to its original form.*

To make your *cryptosystem* even tougher to crack, you can add a *key*. This is an extra step or two in the cipher that's not in the cipher program but stored somewhere else—on the computer or in your head. Why a key? A key makes the cipher program useless to anyone who runs it without your approval. This might be a family member snooping around your private letters, or an information burglar trying to decipher your family's records.

What is a key? A key can either be a *password* or *passwords* (like "Open Sesame"), or it can be an *extra step in the cipher*. Every time the cipher is run, it only goes so far before it asks for the key—a key that only you know. If it doesn't get the key, it doesn't work, and it stops running. A simple key for the system above could be:

> After the 1's and 0's are
> reversed, flip each byte over
> backward.

This creates new bytes that are the mirror images of your original, encrypted bytes. To see how this works, let's take a single letter—the "D" from "Dear"—and see what happens to it. Originally, the "D" is stored as an ASCII byte in the computer's memory. It looks like this: "01000100." After the cipher program runs, the "D" looks like this: "10111011." Before the program is through, however, it types a message on the screen, asking you for the key. The key is in the form of a few extra commands to the computer. You type the commands into the computer, the cipher program processes them, and the "D" changes again. Now it looks like this: "11011101."† It would take a pretty smart information thief to make any sense out of your letter now.

GETTING STARTED

There are many ways to write a cipher program and a cryptanalyst program. A lot of the challenge comes from figuring out a way on your

---

* Remember, this example, although effective, is quite simple. It is important for you to read more on the subject before you try anything involving your family's important records.

† This byte is interpreted by most printers and terminals as a right bracket—"]."

own. To invent a simple cryptosystem, you can use *BASIC*, or any of the other high-level languages. One way to write a system in *BASIC* would be to set up a *table of bytes*—or *letters*. Associated with each byte in the table would be the encoded byte—the one that's flipped, reversed, or whatever. When your program reads a document, like a private letter, it would take each byte, feed it into the table, get back an encoded byte, and substitute it for the original.

How much *BASIC*, for example, do you need to know to be able to write a cipher program? You will need to know the "Ten Commands" (see the chapter titled "You're Trapped!"). You should also learn about the "DIM" command, which enables you to set up your table; and commands like "CHR$" and "ASC" which let you treat ASCII bytes as decimal numbers, and vice versa. Once the byte is a number, you can do arithmetic on it and really create a complicated secret code—one that would be very difficult to crack.‡

Finally, if you are serious about ciphers, secret codes, and cryptosystems, you should learn some *assembly language* (see the chapter titled "A Whirlwind Tour."). Assembly language lets you manipulate individual bits inside a byte. Using assembly language, some arithmetic, and a little ingenuity, you can come up with a sophisticated secret code.

‡ See Appendix A for books on *BASIC*.

BUILD A
COMPUTER
WATCHDOG

N ot everybody is impressed with home computers. Here are some typical comments:

"Home computers are a solution looking for a problem."

"The only jobs a home computer can do are trivial."

"They're nothing but expensive toys!"

Are home computers just toys? Isn't there something useful they can do? In this chapter and the next two chapters, you take a look at areas where home computers can do a job that's not just useful, it's invaluable. First you'll see how a home computer can act as a watchdog and guard your home. Next, you'll watch how you and a home computer might save a family member's life. Third, you'll learn how a home computer could enrich the life of one of your handicapped friends.

CAUGHT BY A COMPUTER

The night is pitch black. The luxurious country home is dark and empty. "Picking this lock will be a snap," whispers the burglar to his companion. A moment later, the two are inside the house. The family silver, china, electric appliances, and jewelry are practically in arm's reach. "We're going to make a killing," the other burglar whispers.

"STOP WHERE YOU ARE!!" booms a police bullhorn. A siren screams. Tires screech. "HANDS OVER YOUR HEAD!!"

The astonished burglars jerk their arms into the air. "How . . . how did you know we were here?" one of them asks. "There's nobody around for miles."

"Nobody human," a policeman says with a chuckle. "You were caught by a computer."

Scenes like this might be taking place in homes all across America. Families are programming their home computers to warn them about burglars, fire, and other emergencies. The computers are sounding alarms, calling the police or fire department, and taking other emergency action.

A *watchdog computer* can be a small unit that does only one thing: look for trouble twenty-four hours a day. Or it can be a regular home computer with multiprogramming. *Multiprogramming* means that the computer can process more than one program at the same time. Your computer could have a watchdog program running through it all the time, yet still have enough power to let you do anything else you wanted to.

Like a robot, a watchdog computer needs to be aware of its environment. To give the computer "eyes" and "ears," you need to tie it into a network of *snooper circuits* called *sensors*. The sensors can detect suspicious sounds, lights, motion, or pressure. There are *infrared* sensors to detect sound, light, and motion; *ultrasonic* sensors to detect motion; *pressure switches* to sense someone's footsteps on the stairs; *photoelectric devices* to sense movement; and *contact sensors* to signal you that someone is opening a door or a window.

The computer watchdog could also have various alarms, including bedroom display panels with buzzers and blinking lights, loud horns and bells, floodlights, ceiling water sprinklers, and an automatic phone-dialing device to alert the police.

Most important, a computer watchdog is smart: It can make decisions. For example, when the computer detects someone in the house, it knows whether it is a burglar, or just you, your family, or one of your friends. Likewise, if you were having a barbecue and smoke from the burning charcoal blew into the house, the computer wouldn't douse the inside of your house with water sprinklers. Further, if the computer had some of its wires cut, it would automatically know which ones and tell you by displaying their names and locations on the picture screen. Finally, the computer would record all events during an emergency. After the emergency was over, it could do an *instant replay* of the entire sequence of events—before and after the alarm.

There are many commercial home-security systems available that run on a computer, but they cost a lot of money. Setting up a home-security system on your own could be much cheaper and a real challenge.* Once you turned your computer into a watchdog, you might be interested in teaching it some extra tricks. Some ideas: You can have the watchdog

---

* Home-computer magazines often carry articles on home-security computers. See Appendix B.

make it appear that you're at home when you go on vacation. How? Program the watchdog to turn lights on and off randomly in the evening, then turn all lights off later in the night or in the following morning. Or program your watchdog to talk on the telephone. You can get it to answer calls when you are away from home, and make emergency phone calls in a fraction of a second.

Remember, every electrical appliance in your home can be tied into a home computer. It's up to you to decide which appliances give your computer watchdog its *teeth*.

SAVE
A LIFE

Let's say your parents are out, and you're baby-sitting your little sister. You walk into the kitchen and can't believe your eyes: Your sister has just swallowed half a bottle of XYZ cleaning fluid. She begins gagging and crying. You grab the bottle. The label's partly missing— you can't find the antidote. What can you give her? She looks really bad.

You run into the living room, switch on your home computer, and push the RESET button. Two seconds later the *POISON* program automatically comes on the screen. It flashes the phone numbers of your community's poison-control unit, your family doctor, and the hospital emergency room. One of your friends is at your house, helping you baby-sit. You have her start making calls.

You type a "1," and the *POISON* program asks you what your sister swallowed. You type in the name "XYZ," the program searches its files, and only a second later, it tells you: "Get water or milk into poison victim fast!"

You dash back into the kitchen and manage to get two glasses of water into your sister before the poison-control unit arrives. They rush off with her. Half an hour later you get a call: Your sister is okay—thanks to you, your friend, and the home computer.

The *POISON* program is available from Berkeley Medical Associates.* It will run on most major home computers. For purposes of speed, it is stored on disk. Even though as many as twenty-four hundred poisons and antidotes can be listed and searched, it takes the program less than six seconds—at most!—to give you an answer.

---

* Berkeley Medical Associates, Inc., P. O. Box 5279, Berkeley, CA 94705 (415-653-6707).

The goal of the program's designers was the swift retrieval of accurate, helpful information. No wonder. More than three thousand people in the United States die from poisoning each year, most of them under the age of five. Many of these people would not have died had they gotten help more swiftly.

But don't stop here. The *POISON* program can just be the start. There are many emergencies that commonly occur around the home, including burns, shock, choking, wounds, broken bones, convulsions, etc. With the right programs, your computer can be a life saver. But should you write the programs yourself? Probably not—at least at first. Stick to well-known, thoroughly tested, canned programs (like *POISON*) until you get to be a very good programmer. Programs that provide information in an emergency must work perfectly—the first time, every time.

So what can you do? Make it *your* job to study computer magazines and track down all the canned emergency programs.† Get hold of the

† See Appendix B.

programs, get them running on your computer, and enter all of the emergency information—antidotes, treatments, phone numbers, etc. Do some practice sessions on the computer to make sure everything is running smoothly. Then call in your family and teach them the basics on what to do in case of emergency. Last and most important, keep all the information up to date, and hold frequent emergency drills to keep everyone's memory fresh. All of this takes patience and hard work, but the benefits are worth it: You and your computer could save someone's life.

HELP
A FRIEND

Imagine for a moment that you are deaf. What's it like? When you turn on the TV, you can't hear the sound. The radio and the telephone are totally useless. Even a simple conversation with your family or friends is difficult. There is nothing to hear: no music, no crying, no laughter.

Or what if you lost your eyesight? Or your voice? Or you became paralyzed from the waist up? How would you communicate with the world? *You might use a home computer.* It can be "eyes" for people who cannot see, "ears" for people who cannot hear, a "voice" for those who cannot talk, and arms and legs for people with motor disabilities.

Many companies make special-purpose computers especially designed for people with handicaps. For example, there is the Kurzweil Reading Machine, a computer for blind people that will "read" a printed page and say the words it sees. Another company, Telesensory Systems, has already sold thousands of talking calculators.

Another group of companies—including Votrax and HC Electronics —produce a voice synthesizer called *The Phonic Mirror*, which is used by persons with speech impediments. The people cannot talk properly, but they can use the *Mirror* to speak for them. For example, they might push a button that says, "Come here." Inside the *Mirror*, a program translates the signal from the button into audible speech.

The *Mirror* can also be used by people even more severely handicapped. Switches can be added to enable someone to use body or eye movements—or even their breath!—to activate the *Mirror*. Using the *Mirror*, people who are almost totally paralyzed have regained their ability to speak.

Another computer is equally remarkable: the *TS-100A Microcomputer*, manufactured by Computers for the Physically Handicapped, Inc.

The *TS-100A* can be mounted on a table or on a wheelchair. The switch that controls the computer comes with attachments so that the handicapped person can operate it with only a slight motion from almost any part of his or her body. Nine verbal programs come with the *TS-100A*, including a twelve-hundred-word vocabulary, single-letter spelling, tutoring, a selection of phrases the person frequently uses, and even an *electronic notebook* for writing letters, writing notes, and sending messages. Accessories can be attached that allow the person to answer a telephone, turn pages in a book, and, by remote control, operate almost any electrical appliance in the house. When it is turned on, the computer displays a *menu* of functions on the screen. The names of the functions (like "Phrases," "Spelling," "Tutoring," and "Notebook") appear on the screen, one at a time. The person selects a particular function by pressing the switch when he or she sees the function wanted.

A third device is the *C-Phone* made by C-Phone, Inc. The *C-Phone* is to replace the relatively expensive and bulky *teletypes* (TTYs) that deaf people have used over the years as a means for carrying on phone conversations. The *C-Phone* is cheap, light, and has many special features. For example, there is a BLANK key that a hearing-impaired person uses at the end of each of his messages. It says, "I am finished. Your turn." Another feaure: The *C-Phone* lets a person compose his message before he makes the call. This is especially useful for making expensive long-distance calls. Finally, the *C-Phone* comes with a sound-sensing device that blinks a light whenever a deaf person receives an incoming phone call.

The *C-Phone* is really a little computer. A deaf person can use a *C-Phone* and dial in to *DEAFNET*, a computer network that links people in several cities, including Washington, D.C., Boston, and San Francisco. A central computer on *DEAFNET* co-ordinates all calls and provides a wide range of services. For an example, let's take a deaf person in Framingham, Massachusetts, who uses *C-Phone* to get a *mailbox* message stored on the computer. The message was left several days earlier by a deaf friend in Washington, D.C., who was using an old-model TTY. After getting her mail the person calls the *DEAFNET* computer for a printout of the local news, weather, and traffic conditions. Later in the day, she calls the computer and participates in a conference on deaf people's problems. That night after dinner, she uses *DEAFNET* to attend (by phone) a class on American history.

DO IT YOURSELF

Handicapped people have special problems and needs when it comes to using a computer. Do they need specially designed computers? Frequently not. Take the story of Peter, a ten-year-old Australian boy.

The *Phonic Mirror HandiVoice* is a "home" computer that talks for nonverbal people—victims of cerebral palsy, spinal-cord injuries, multiple sclerosis, or cancer of the voice box or tongue. In the picture above, a therapist is helping a nonverbal person program a *HandiVoice* to combine *phonemes* (word sounds) into actual words. [Courtesy of Votrax (a division of Federal Screw Works), HC Electronics, and the United Cerebral Palsy Center of Syracuse, New York.]

Peter is smart, but until recently he couldn't read because he is *dyslexic*. Somehow the letters in the words he read got all scrambled. Now, using a *TRS-80* computer from Radio Shack, Peter is learning to read. The computer prints words, one at a time, from a basic word list. Using arrows that move from left to right, the computer prompts Peter to read each word, letter by letter, from left to right. The computer also acts as a *reading pacer*, or *rabbit*. When Peter first began using the computer, it flashed words on the screen at a rate of twenty words a minute. Working slowly and patiently, Peter has gradually improved his reading speed to better than fifty words a minute.

There is also John Watkin's daughter, Dawn, a victim of cerebral palsy. After she contracted the disease, Dawn was unable to hold a pencil and write her name. She was cut off. She couldn't communicate.

Dawn's father sought desperately for a new way for Dawn to communicate—to share her thoughts and feelings with family and friends. After considerable effort, he developed an extra-large flat computer keyboard that Dawn was able to use. He was thrilled the first time Dawn spelled out her name on the computer screen.

And there's Tim Scully's friend Robin. Scully is a prisoner in a federal penitentiary. His friend Robin has cerebral palsy so bad that the only part of her body she can control is one of her knees. Robin's prison is no less real than the one holding her friend.

Scully set out to find a way to help Robin. He designed a knee switch hooked to a computer that allows Robin to "talk" by selecting from a menu of words displayed on the screen. Before, Robin couldn't even ask for a drink of water. Now, thanks to her friend, she can carry on a conversation and stay in touch with the world around her.

If you have a friend or family member who has a handicap, tell him or her about home computers. Think of ways to help the person use a home computer personally. If the person is deaf, see if he or she can use the computer to tie into *DEAFNET*.

Look through computer magazines and you will find several articles and ads on ways home computers can help a handicapped person.* For a project, you could buy or make the parts your friend needs to operate the computer. Then write programs for your friend to use. Even better, teach him or her how to program. If you are successful, you will have forged a new link between your friend and the world. It's a link of two-way communication that could enrich your friend's life.

* See Appendix B.

GATEWAY
TO THE
UNIVERSE

As you have seen in this book, home computers can be useful, practical, entertaining, and educational. But perhaps most important of all, *they are tools to help you build models.* Now or sometime soon, using a home computer, you'll be able to type in the notes of a song, modify it, and have the computer synthesize the sound of an entire orchestra. You'll use a light pen to draw a sketch on the screen, then expand your simple drawing into a three-dimensional, animated picture in full color. In each case, you will be using the computer to model, or simulate, the world—the real world or an imaginary world you dream up. And it will do it beautifully and convincingly—but only after you understand the world enough to describe it to the computer.

You can use your models like Albert Einstein used *thought experiments:* to explore the impossible, to imagine the unimaginable. You can speed up time, then slow it down or make it go backward. You can make gravity push up, not pull down. You can draw a spaceship and make it go faster than light; or you can create an ice age and watch glaciers scratch their way across the world, then retreat. You can build a model of the continents drifting over the earth, across millions of years. You can model an earthquake, a volcano, a thunderstorm. You can model a feudal village in the Middle Ages, or a tree that grows from acorn to sapling to giant oak in seconds. You can follow the lifespan of a subatomic neutrino, or a muon, or a pion. You can stretch out their lives and follow their trails.

Remember: A home computer's hardware is governed by certain laws (electrons must flow along given wires), but the computer models you build—all your games and your projects—are limited only by what you can learn and how much you can imagine. You can learn a lot. You can imagine more. Just start by asking, "What if . . . ?"

HOME-COMPUTER BOOKS

Home computers are changing so fast that many home-computer books are outdated almost as soon as they are published. If you want to keep up with home-computer developments, the best strategy is to subscribe to a couple of home-computer magazines (see Appendix B) and get on all the catalog mailing lists (see Appendix C). You'll hear about new ideas, new programs, new computers, new equipment, and new books as soon as they appear. In the meantime, here are some good, recent books, grouped by subject:

Introduction to Home Computers

BALL, MARION J., AND CHARP, SYLVIA. *Be a Computer Literate.* Morristown, N.J.: Creative Computing Press, 1977.

BUCKWALTER, LEN. *The Home Computer Book.* New York: Pocket Books, 1979.

BUNNELL, DAVID. *Personal Computing: A Beginner's Guide.* New York: Hawthorne Books, 1978.

MOODY, ROBERT. *The First Book of Microcomputers.* Rochelle Park, N.J.: Hayden Book Company, 1978.

OSBORNE, ADAM. *An Introduction to Microcomputers (Volume 0: The Beginner's Book).* Berkeley, Calif.: Adam Osborne and Associates, 1977.

————. *An Introduction to Microcomputers (Volume 1: Basic Concepts).* Berkeley, Calif.: Adam Osborne and Associates, 1976.

SOLOMON, LESLIE, AND VEIT, STANLEY. *Getting Involved with Your Own*

Computer: A Guide for Beginners. Short Hills, N.J.: Ridley Enslow, Publishers, 1977.

SPENCER, DONALD D. *Microcomputers at a Glance.* New York: Camelot (Avon), 1977.

WALTER, RUSS. *Secret Guide to Computers.* 92 Botolph Street, Boston, Mass. Russ Walter, 1980.

Computers and Society

BAER, ROBERT M. *The Digital Villain.* Reading, Mass.: Addison-Wesley Publishing Company, 1972.

BARRON, IANN, AND CURNOW, RAY. *The Future with Microelectronics: Forecasting the Effects of Information Technology.* New York: Nichols Publishing Company, 1979.

DERTOUZOS, MICHAEL L., AND MOSS, JOEL, eds. *The Computer Age: A Twenty-year View.* Cambridge, Mass.: MIT Press, 1979.

GEORGE, FRANK. *Machine Takeover: The Growing Threat to Human Freedom in a Computer-Controlled Society.* Elmsford, New York: Pergamon Press Inc., 1977.

GRAHAM, NEILL. *The Mind Tool: Computers and Their Impact on Society.* St. Paul, Minn.: West Publishing Company, 1980.

WEINER, NORBERT. *The Human Use of Human Beings: Cybernetics and Society.* New York: Avon Books, 1967.

WEIZENBAUM, JOSEPH. *Computer Power and Human Reason: From Judgment to Calculation.* San Francisco, Calif.: W. H. Freeman & Company, 1976.

The *BASIC* Computer Language

ALBRECHT, BOB. *My Computer Likes Me When I Speak in BASIC.* Menlo Park, Calif.: Dymax, 1972.

ALBRECHT, BOB; FINKEL, LEROY; AND BROWN, JERALD R. *BASIC for Home Computers: A Self-teaching Guide.* New York: John Wiley & Sons, 1978.

DWYER, THOMAS A., AND CRITCHFIELD, MARGOT. *BASIC and the Personal Computer.* Reading, Mass.: Addison-Wesley Publishing Company, 1978.

NAGIN, PAUL, AND LEDGARD, HENRY F. *BASIC with Style: Programming Proverbs.* Rochelle Park, N.J.: Hayden Book Company, 1978.

SPENCER, DONALD D. *Sixty Challenging Problems with BASIC Solutions.* Ormond Beach, Fla.: Camelot Publishing Company, 1977.

PASCAL

BOWLES, KENNETH L. *Microcomputer Problem Solving Using PASCAL.* New York: Springer-Verlag, 1977.

CONWAY, RICHARD A. *A Primer on PASCAL.* Cambridge, Mass.: Winthrop Publishers (a subsidiary of Prentice-Hall), 1976.

FINDLAY, W., AND WATT, DAVID A. *PASCAL: An Introduction to Methodical Programming.* Washington, D.C.: Computer Science Press, 1978.

GROGONO, PETER. *Programming in PASCAL.* Reading, Mass.: Addison-Wesley Publishing Company, 1978.

LIFFICK, BLAISE W., ed. *The BYTE Book of PASCAL.* Peterborough, N.H.: BYTE Publications, 1980.

WELSH, JIM, AND ELDER, JOHN. *Introduction to PASCAL.* Englewood Cliffs, N.J.: Prentice-Hall, 1979.

Games

AHL, DAVID H., ed. *BASIC Computer Games: Microcomputer Edition.* Morristown, N.J.: Creative Computing Press, 1978.

———. *More BASIC Computer Games.* Morristown, N.J.: Creative Computing Press, 1979.

EMMERICHS, JACK. *SuperWumpus.* Peterborough, N.H.: BYTE Publications, 1978.

GARRETT, ROGER. *Starship Simulation.* Forest Grove, Ore.: Dilithium Press, 1978.

PEOPLE'S COMPUTER COMPANY. *What to Do After You Hit Return or PCC's First Book of Computer Games.* Menlo Park, Calif.: People's Computer Company, 1975.

SAGE, EDWIN R. *Fun and Games with the Computer.* Newburyport, Mass.: ENTELEK, 1975.

SPENCER, DONALD D. *Fun with Computers and BASIC.* New York: Camelot (Avon), 1977.

———. *Game Playing with BASIC.* Rochelle Park, N.J.: Hayden Book Company, 1977.

Chess

FREY, PETER, ed. *Chess Skill in Man and Machine.* New York: Springer-Verlag, 1976.

LEVY, DAVID. *Chess and Computers*. Washington, D.C.: Computer Science Press, 1976.

NEWBORN, MONROE. *Computer Chess*. New York: Academic Press, 1975.

SPRACKLEN, DAN, AND SPRACKLEN, KATHE. *SARGON: A Computer Chess Program*. Rochelle Park, N.J.: Hayden Book Company, 1978.

Projects

HEISERMAN, DAVID L. *How to Design and Build Your Own Custom TV Games*. Blue Ridge Summit, Pa.: TAB Books, 1978.

PUOTINEN, C. J. *Computing Horoscopes with Your Electronic Calculator*. Hoboken, N.J.: Ninth Sign Publications, 1978.

SEVENTY-THREE MAGAZINE EDITORS. *The Giant Handbook of Computer Projects*. Blue Ridge Summit, Pa.: TAB Books, 1979.

SPENCER, DONALD D. *The Computer Quiz Book*. New York: Camelot (Avon), 1978.

Models and Simulation

ABT, CLARK. *Serious Games*. New York: The Viking Press, 1970.

BOOCOOK, SARANE, AND SCHILD, E. O. *Simulation Games in Learning*. Beverly Hills, Calif.: Sage, 1978.

DUKE, RICHARD, ed. *Learning with Simulations and Games*. Beverly Hills, Calif.: Sage, 1978.

LEWIS, THEODORE, AND SMITH, BRIAN J. *Computer Principles of Modeling and Simulation*. Boston, Mass.: Houghton Mifflin Company, 1979.

O'DONOVAN, THOMAS. *GPSS: Simulation Made Simple*. New York: John Wiley & Sons, 1979.

Robots

GEORGE, F. H., AND HUMPHRIES, J. D., eds. *The Robots Are Coming*. London, England: NCC Publications, 1974.

HEISERMAN, DAVID L. *Build Your Own Working Robot*. Blue Ridge Summit, Pa.: TAB Books, 1976.

LOOFBOURROW, TOD. *How to Build a Computer-controlled Robot*. Rochelle Park, N.J.: Hayden Book Company, 1978.

REICHARDT, JASIA. *Robots: Fact, Fiction, and Prediction*. Harmondsworth, Middlesex, England: Penguin Books, 1978.

WINKLESS, NELS, AND BROWNING, IBEN. *Robots on Your Doorstep* (*A Book about Thinking Machines*). Portland, Ore.: Robotics Press, 1978.

YOUNG, JOHN F. *Robotics*. New York: John Wiley & Sons, 1973.

Music

ANDERTON, CRAIG. *Electronic Projects for Musicians*. Cupertino, Calif.: Guitar Player, 1975.

BACKUS, JOHN. *The Acoustical Foundations of Music*, 2nd ed. New York: W. W. Norton & Company, 1977.

HILLER, L. A., AND ISAACSON, LEONARD M. *Experimental Music: Composition with an Electronic Computer*. Westport, Conn.: Greenwood Press, 1979.

LINCOLN, HARRY B. *The Computer and Music*. Ithaca, N.Y.: Cornell University Press, 1970.

MATHEWS, MAX. *The Technology of Computer Music*. Cambridge, Mass.: MIT Press, 1969.

MORGAN, CHRISTOPHER. *The BYTE Book of Computer Music*. Peterborough, N.H.: BYTE Publications, 1978.

Graphics and Art

CHASEN, SYLVAN H. *Geometric Principles and Procedures for Computer Graphics Applications*. Englewood Cliffs, N.J.: Prentice-Hall, 1980.

FRANKE, HERBERT W. *Computer Graphics—Computer Art*, trans. Gustave Metzger. London, England: Phaidon, 1971.

HALAS, JOHN, ed. *Computer Animation*. New York: Focal Press (distributed by Hastings House Publications), 1974.

LEAVITT, RUTH. *Artist and Computer*. New York: Harmony Books (distributed by Crown Publishers), 1976.

NEWMAN, WILLIAM N., AND SPROULL, ROBERT F. *Principles of Interactive Computer Graphics*. New York: McGraw-Hill, 1976.

PECKHAM, HERBERT. *Computer Graphics*. Palo Alto, Calif.: The Scientific Press, 1974.

Schoolwork

CAUCHON, PAUL. *Chemistry with a Computer*. Newburyport, Mass.: ENTELEK, 1976.

Computer Crime

BEQUAI, AUGUST. *Computer Crime.* Lexington, Mass.: D. C. Heath & Company, 1978.

CUNNINGHAM, JOHN E. *Security Electronics,* 2nd ed. Indianapolis, Ind.: Howard W. Sams & Company, 1977.

LEIBHOLZ, STEPHEN, AND WILSON, LOUIS D. *User's Guide to Computer Crime.* Radnor, Pa.: Chilton Book Company, 1974.

PARKER, DONN B. *Crime by Computer.* New York: Charles Scribner's Sons, 1976.

WHITESIDE, THOMAS. *Computer Capers.* New York: Mentor, 1978.

Novels, Poetry, and Stories

CHARBONNEAU, LOUIS. *The Intruder.* Garden City, N.Y.: Doubleday & Company, 1979.

GERROLD, DAVID. *When Harlie Was One.* New York: Ballantine Books, 1975.

MCNEIL, JOHN. *The Consultant.* New York: Ballantine Books, 1978.

PAULSEN, GARY. *Compkill.* New York: Dell Publishing Company, 1979.

RYAN, THOMAS J. *The Adolescence of P-1.* New York: Collier Books, 1977.

VAN TASSEL, DENNIE, ed. *Computers, Computers, Computers: In Fiction and in Verse.* Nashville, Tenn.: Thomas Nelson, 1977.

HOME-COMPUTER
MAGAZINES

Home computers are changing so rapidly, it is almost impossible to keep up with all of the new computers, products, games, and programs. But there is a way: *Read the magazines!* Most of the major magazines appear monthly. They have a huge amount of current material in each issue, and their articles and features cover almost all angles of personal computing. Another bonus: Each month, the magazines carry several complete programs that you can copy and run on your home computer.

Here are some of the major home-computer magazines:

BYTE   An invaluable source of state-of-the-art information for the advanced home-computer user. For a single issue or subscription, call (toll-free) 800-258-5485; or write *BYTE* Subscriptions, P. O. Box 390, Martinsville, NJ 08836.

CREATIVE COMPUTING   Attractive, full of cartoons, pictures, games, and projects, and a lot of fun to read. For a single issue or subscription, call (toll-free) 800-631-8112; or write *Creative Computing* magazine, P. O. Box 789-M, Morristown, NJ 07960.

DR. DOBB'S JOURNAL   A wide-ranging "cookbook" of useful programs—listings, documentation, explanations—for the sophisticated home-computer user. For a single issue or for a subscription, call 415-323-3111; or write *Dr. Dobb's Journal of Computer Calisthenics & Orthodontia*, People's Computer Company, P. O. Box E, 1263 El Camino Real, Menlo Park, CA 94025.

INTERFACE AGE   Attractive, easy to read, and full of home and business projects and applications. For a single issue or for a subscription, call 213-926-9540; or write *Interface Age* magazine, 16704 Marquardt Avenue, Cerritos, CA 90701.

MICROCOMPUTING   A grab bag of practical projects and tutorials for the inter-mediate-level home-computer or business-computer user. For a single issue or for a subscription, call 603-924-7296; or write *Microcomputing*, Subscription Department, P. O. Box 997, Farmingdale, NY 11737.

ONCOMPUTING   A good magazine to help you get started. Articles on hard-ware, software, computer basics, and new products. For a single issue or for a subscription, call (toll-free) 800-258-5485; or write *onComputing*, P. O. Box 307, Martinsville, NJ 08836.

PERSONAL COMPUTING   Attractive, fun, easy-to-read articles on home and business projects and on new products. For a single issue or for a subscription, call 617-232-5470; or write Circulation, *Personal Computing*, 1050 Common-wealth Avenue, Boston, MA 02215.

RECREATIONAL COMPUTING   Games, projects, and more games! For a single issue or for a subscription, call 415-323-3111; or write *Recreational Comput-ing*, People's Computer Company, P. O. Box E, 1263 El Camino Real, Menlo Park, CA 94025.

There are dozens of other magazines, bulletins, and newsletters put out by local computer clubs and by the users and manufacturers of specific models of home computers. For example, there is *80 Microcom-puting* (Subscription Services Department, *80 Microcomputing*, P. O. Box 981, Farmingdale, NY 11737), which is devoted to programs and products for owners of Radio Shack's *TRS-80* home computer; and *IRIDIS* and *CURSOR*, monthly "cassette" magazines of programs for the *Atari 400* and the *Commodore PET* (same address for both: P. O. Box 550, Goleta, CA 93017). To find out more about all of these publica-tions, visit your local computer store (look in the Yellow Pages under "Computers" or "Data Processing"), or call or write the manufacturer of your computer.

There are also dozens of special-interest magazines on specific sub-jects. For example, if you are interested in robots, there is an excellent magazines called *Robotics Age* (P. O. Box 4029, Houston, TX 77210). If you have a special interest in computer music, get a subscription to the *Journal of Computer Music* (People's Computer Company, P. O. Box E, 1263 El Camino Real, Menlo Park, CA 94025). If you like computer video, movies, graphics, and games, try *Inovision* (from the Inovision Club, P. O. Box 400040, Dallas, TX 75240) or *Video* (Reese Publishing Company, 235 Park Avenue South, New York, NY 10003).

Also, there are several "Handbooks" on personal computers pub-lished by the editors of such magazines as *Popular Mechanics*, *Mechanix Illustrated*, *Elementary Electronics*, *Consumer's Guide*, and so on. These handbooks appear once or twice a year, are reasonably current, and give you a quick introduction to home computers. The handbooks are cheap, and are sold at almost any big newstand. If you are just getting started, they make a good buy.

Further, if you want to keep up with what's happening in home computers, but you can't afford a subscription to all the magazines, get the latest *Periodical Guide for Computerists* by E. Berg (E. Berg Publications), available through *BITS*, the microcomputer books clearinghouse (25 Route 101 West, P. O. Box 428, Peterborough, NH 03458). The *Periodical Guide* lists, by subject, all articles on microcomputers appearing during the previous year in over twenty-seven different publications. It is especially helpful if you are intersted in tracking down all the recent articles on a particular subject, like computer art, secret codes, or robots.

If you can't afford Berg's book, you might consider writing each of the magazines for their *Cumulative Index and Reprint Catalog*. This is usually available free and is a list of all articles ever published in the magazine, grouped together by subject.

Finally, if you want to know about home-computer news as soon as it breaks, then you need a home-computer newspaper, like *InfoWorld*. (Write Circulation Department, *InfoWorld*, 375 Cochituate Road, Route 30, Framingham, MA 01701). *InfoWorld* comes out biweekly (twice a month) and carries the latest developments and gossip about who's doing what in home computers.

HOME-COMPUTER CATALOGS

Home-Computer Books

There are dozens of books on home computers. Unfortunately, since home computers are changing so fast, most of the books are already outdated. This is why it is important to find out about the new books as soon as they appear. There are several ways to do this: First, you can read the book ads and the "Review" section in your home-computer magazines. Second, you can browse through copies of *Books in Print* and *Forthcoming Books* at your local bookstore or library. Third, and easiest, you can get on the mailing list for the home-computer book publishers and clearinghouses, including:

BITS Publishes a catalog two to four times a year that contains hundreds of titles from over fifty different publishers. For a copy of the catalog, call (toll-free) 800-258-5477; or write BITS, 25 Route 101 West, P. O. Box 428, Peterborough, NH 03458.

BYTE BOOKS Publishes a catalog of PAPERBYTE and BYTE BOOKS. For a copy of this catalog, call (toll-free) 800-258-5485; or write BYTE BOOKS Division, 70 Main Street, Peterborough, NH 03458.

CREATIVE COMPUTING BOOK SERVICE Publishes the *Creative Computing Catalogue*. For a copy of this catalog, call (toll-free) 800-631-8112; or write Creative Computing Book Service, P. O. Box 789-M, Morristown, NJ 07960.

DILITHIUM PRESS Publishes a catalog of all of its books on home computers. Write to Dilithium Press, P. O. Box 92, Forest Grove, OR 97116.

HAYDEN BOOK COMPANY Publishes a catalog of all of its books on home computers. Write to Hayden Book Company, 50 Essex Street, Rochelle Park, NJ 07662.

OSBORNE & ASSOCIATES Publishes a catalog of all its books on home computers. Write to Osborne & Associates, 630 Bancroft Way, Dept. W14, Berkeley, CA 94710.

PRENTICE-HALL Publishes a catalog of all of its books on computers. Write to Prentice-Hall, Englewood Cliffs, NJ 07632.

SYBEX Publishes a catalog of all of its books on home computers. Write to Sybex, Dept. B11, 2020 Milvia Street, Berkeley, CA 94704.

TAB BOOKS Publishes a catalog of all of its books. Write to TAB Books, Blue Ridge Summit, PA 17214.

Computers, Parts, and Equipment

ADVANCED COMPUTER PRODUCTS Publishes a catalog of all its products. Write to Advanced Computer Products, P. O. Box 17329, Irvine, CA 92713.

COMPUTERLAND Publishes a catalog of all its products. Write to ComputerLand, 14400 Catalina Street, San Leandro, CA 94577.

HOBBY WORLD Publishes a catalog of all its products. Write to Hobby World, 19511 Business Center Drive, Northridge, CA 91324.

MINIMICROMART Publishes a catalog of all its products. Write to MiniMicro-Mart, 1618 James Street, Syracuse, NY 13203.

NEWMAN COMPUTER EXCHANGE Publishes a catalog of all its products. Write to NCE/CompuMart, Inc., P. O. Box 8610, 1250 North Main Street, Ann Arbor, MI 48107.

Computer Games and Other Programs

Creative Computing, Osborne & Associates, and Hayden each publish a catalog on computer games and software. For their address, see above (in the section "Home-Computer Books"). You can also get catalogs from:

PERSONAL SOFTWARE For a catalog, write to Personal Software, Inc., 592 Weddell Drive, Sunnyvale, CA 94086.

RAINBOW COMPUTING For a catalog, write to Rainbow Computing, Inc., 10723 White Oak Avenue, Granada Hills, CA 91344.

SCIENTIFIC RESEARCH A software firm that produces programs for home-computer users. Write to Roger W. Brown, President, Scientific Research, 220 Knollwood, Key Biscayne, FL 33149.

THE SOURCE A "department store" full of computer programs. Write to The Source, Telecommunications Corporation of America, 1616 Anderson Road, McLean, VA 22102.

BEFORE YOU BUY
A HOME COMPUTER ...

When you and your family finally decide to get a home computer, you will want to run right out and buy one. But first, just to be safe, you should spend some time comparing the different computers. Visit computer stores, talk to your friends and teachers, and look at some magazines and books (see Appendixes A and B). Which home computers have the features *you* want? Here is a checklist to help you compare different computers:

1. How much does the computer cost? (Is it within the family's budget?)

2. What parts *don't* come with the computer for the basic price? (The video terminal? The tape recorder? The *BASIC* monitor/interpreter?)

3. Can you take the computer home with you from the store, or do you have to wait for a new one to be shipped? If so, how long must you wait?

4. How many computers of this type have already been sold? Any major problems? Minor problems? Quirks?

5. If your computer breaks down once you've got it home, who will fix it:
   a. *The manufacturer?* (Is he local? Is there a *warranty?* If so, for what parts, and for how long?)
   b. *The computer store?* (For how much?)
   c. *You?* (How?)

6. Is the computer easy to set up? Turn on and off? Operate? Program?

7. What do you want to do first when you get the computer home? Can *this* computer do that?

8. What would you like to try later? (Remember: What if . . . ?) Can *this* computer do that, too?

9. Can the computer be expanded? Can you add memory? A disk drive? Voice recognition? Can you make it talk? Play music? Can it make noises? (a *must* for games).

10. When you add new parts to the computer, can you plug them right in, or do you need special *interface boards* and other costly extras?

11. Can the computer do *graphics* (pictures)? Try it out. Does it make high-resolution graphics (for smooth, realistic pictures), or low-resolution graphics (for jagged, blocklike pictures)? Are there a wide range of graphics characters on the keyboard? Does the computer let you define new characters?

12. Can the computer make *color* pictures? How many colors? How many different levels of brightness?

13. Does the computer come with game paddles and game controls? (If not, are they available, and how much extra do they cost?)

14. Is the computer's brain—its CPU, or Central Processing Unit—an older eight-bit processor, or one of the newer, more powerful sixteen-bit processors?

15. Can you program the computer yourself? If so, what programming languages (compilers, interpreters, assemblers, and operating systems) come with the computer when you buy it? What additional languages are available?

16. Is *BASIC, PASCAL,* or some equivalent language stored in ROM (Read Only Memory), or must you copy it in from tape or disk each time you use it? Is the computer's control program (the monitor or operating system) stored in ROM?

17. What *canned games* are available? Test them. Are they fun? Easy to use? Are more on the way?

18. Do the canned games and canned programs come on ROM *packs* or *bubble-memory packs* that you can plug into the computer?

19. Are there books and manuals that show you how to use the computer? Look at them. Are they complete and easy to read?

After using the checklist and comparing all the computers, talk over the choices with your family and decide on a *best buy.* Then go out and get your new computer!

ASCII CODING CHART*

ASCII Byte (8 Bits)	Decimal Number
00110000	0
00110001	1
00110010	2
00110011	3
00110100	4
00110101	5
00110110	6
00110111	7
00111000	8
00111001	9

ASCII Byte (8 Bits)	Capital Letters	ASCII Byte (8 Bits)	Lower-case Letters
01000001	A	01100001	a
01000010	B	01100010	b
01000011	C	01100011	c
01000100	D	01100100	d
01000101	E	01100101	e
01000110	F	01100110	f
01000111	G	01100111	g
01001000	H	01101000	h
01001001	I	01101001	i
01001010	J	01101010	j
01001011	K	01101011	k
01001100	L	01101100	l
01001101	M	01101101	m
01001110	N	01101110	n
01001111	O	01101111	o
01010000	P	01110000	p
01010001	Q	01110001	q
01010010	R	01110010	r
01010011	S	01110011	s
01010100	T	01110100	t
01010101	U	01110101	u
01010110	V	01110110	v
01010111	W	01110111	w
01011000	X	01111000	x
01011001	Y	01111001	y
01011010	Z	01111010	z

* This is only a portion of the complete ASCII Coding Chart. There are also codes for punctuation marks, special characters (like "$" and "%"), and non-printing control signals that can be sent by the computer to the video terminal or printer.

DECIMAL AND BINARY NUMBERS

Decimal Numbers (Base 10)	Binary Numbers (Base 2)
0	0
1	1
2	10
3	11
4	100
5	101
6	110
7	111
8	1000
9	1001
10	1010
11	1011
12	1100
13	1101
14	1110
15	1111
16	10000

GLOSSARY

ADD-ON Accessories or "extras" for your home computer.

ADDRESS The storage location of an item in the computer's memory.

ALGORITHM A list of steps to solve a problem, perform a task, or reach a goal. Before you write a program, sit down and write out an *algorithm*, a list of steps explaining (in English) exactly what you want the program to do. Translate the algorithm from English into computer commands, and you have a program.

ALPHANUMERIC PRINTER A device that prints letters, numbers, punctuation marks, and special symbols (like "$," "%," and "&"), but does not print graphics characters—specially shaped symbols you use to draw pictures.

ANALOG-TO-DIGITAL (A–D) CONVERTER A device that takes an electrical charge and transforms it into a *digital* charge—a high charge to signify a "1" or a low or zero charge to signify a "0." Home computers process and store commands and information as a series of digital charges (or *bits*). The bits are grouped together, eight at a time, into *bytes*.

ANALOG SIGNAL A continuous electrical signal that is an exact reproduction of something (like temperature, the position of game-control paddles or sound waves) appearing outside the home computer. Unlike a digital signal (which must be *high* or *low*, *on* or *off*), an analog signal can be any frequency, size, or strength.

APL "A Programming Language." Developed by Kenneth Iverson in the early 1960s. APL is usually implemented as an interpreter. APL commands are brief, powerful, and look like mathematical expressions. APL is a good language to use for solving math, science, or logic problems.

APPLICATION PROGRAM When *you* write a program to run on your home computer, it is an *application* program. It's a program that plays a game, solves a problem, or does a job *you* want done.

ARTIFICIAL INTELLIGENCE Ability of a machine (like a robot or a computer) to imitate a human being in certain areas, like problem solving, decision making, perception, and learning.

ASCII American Standard Code for Information Interchange. Most home computers use ASCII to code all information not used in arithmetic. Letters, numbers (not used in arithmetic), punctuation marks, other characters (like "✕" and "*"), and special control signals are all coded in ASCII. (See Appendix E for a partial ASCII coding chart.)

ASSEMBLY LANGUAGE Developed in the early 1950s so that programmers could use abbreviated-word commands (*pnemonics*) in place of the long, confusing strings of 1's and 0's that form computers' *machine language*. In general, each assembly-language command (like "JMP" or "ADD") translates into a single machine-language command. The program that does the translating is called an *assembler*.

AUDIO DEVICE Any computer device that accepts sound and/or produces sound. Examples include *voice-recognition, music-,* and *speech-synthesis* devices.

BASIC Beginner's All-purpose Symbolic Instruction Code. A *high-level* language developed by John Kemeny and others at Dartmouth College in the mid-1960s. *BASIC* is the most popular home-computer language. It is usually implemented as an *interpreter*, so you can type in commands one at a time, and the computer will obey them instantly.

BAUD Bits of AUdio Data (per second). Used to measure the amount of data sent over a telephone line as two sounds, or tones (a "1" tone and a "0" tone).

BINARY Most home computers are *digital* computers: all their information and commands are in the form of *binary digits* (bits)—"1's" and "0's"—that represent high and low (or on and off) charges of electricity. Numbers and all other information not used in arithmetic are coded in ASCII. Numbers used in arithmetic are coded as *binary* numbers—a way of representing *any* number using only two digits—a "1" and a "0." (See Appendix F for an example of some binary numbers.)

BIT Binary digit. The smallest unit of information inside a home computer. Each bit represents an electrical charge: a "1" represents a high or "on" charge; a "0" represents a low or "off" charge. (See Appendices E and F.)

BUG An error, or mistake, in a computer program.

BUS A wire, or group of wires, inside the computer that act as a path for commands or data (in the form of charges of electricity—bits and bytes) to get from one part of the computer to another.

BYTE A group of eight bits ("1's" and "0's") representing eight charges of electricity. There are different kinds of bytes: *ASCII* bytes, which each represent a letter, number (not used in arithmetic), punctuation mark, etc.; *binary* bytes, which represent numbers used in arithmetic; and *com-*

mand bytes, which represent different machine-language commands to the computer.

CARTRIDGE   A *circuit board* (or card) inside a plastic case with a "plug." On the board are one or more ROM (Read Only Memory) chips. On the chips are programs and information. To get to these *canned* programs or information, you just plug the cartridge into a slot on your home computer.

CHARACTER MATRIX   A big rectangle made up of lots of *little* rectangles. You can make giant (*banner style*) letters and numbers by filling in the appropriate little rectangles.

CHIP   A maze of thousands of miniature wires and circuits, all sitting on a thin slice of silicon the size of your fingernail. There are many different types of chips in a home computer, each with a particular job to do. The main types of chips are: the *CPU* (Central Processing Unit—or brain) chip; the *RAM* (Random Access Memory) chip for storing your programs and information; and the *ROM* (Read Only Memory) chip for storing things like the computer's control program, an interpreter (like *BASIC*), games, etc.

CIRCUIT BOARD   A thin, rectangular plastic board on which are mounted one or more chips. There are many types of circuit boards (also called *PC Boards* and *cards*), including: memory boards, processor boards, I/O (input/output) boards, etc. However, there are also many *single-board* computers in which all major parts of the computer (including its CPU, RAM, and ROM chips) are mounted on one board.

COMMAND TABLE   A list of commands stored in the computer's memory alongside the appropriate *machine-language* instruction. When the computer's brain (or CPU) gets a command, it scans the table. If it finds a command in the table that matches it, it obeys the associated machine-language instruction.

COMMANDS   Orders that you give to the computer in the form of words and numbers typed on a keyboard, words spoken into a microphone, positions of a game paddle or *joystick*, etc.—anything that the computer understands and can obey.

COMMENTS   What happens when you pick up an old program that you haven't looked at in months? Impossible to read or figure out? Not if you remembered to include a lot of comments (in English) before and after all the computer commands. Comments tell you what the computer commands are supposed to do.

COMPILER   The program that takes your commands (written in a *high-level language* like *PASCAL*) and translates them into machine-language instructions that can be processed by the computer. A compiler translates all the commands (in a program) together as a single unit.

COMPUTER   A machine that can accept, remember, and obey a set of commands (a plan or program). A machine that reshapes information. A tool for building models.

CPU Central Processing Unit—the computer's brain. The CPU obeys one machine-language instruction at a time sent to it by its (RAM or ROM) memory. All of the fancy things a home computer does are based on simple logical and arithmetic operations performed inside the CPU.

CRASH When a computer program or computer device stops working—abruptly, unexpectedly, and totally. A crash often results in a loss of data. It can be caused by a device malfunction or a *bug* in a program.

DATA Information stored or processed by the computer.

DIGITAL-TO-ANALOG (D–A) CONVERTER A device that transforms a computer's *digital* (high-low or on-off) electrical pulses to continuous *analog* pulses used to relay information to or power some device outside the computer. (Example: A D–A converter is used to transform computer signals to analog signals that drive a pair of stereo speakers and produce music.)

DIGITIZER An A–D converter that transforms *analog* electrical signals from a TV camera, tracing pen, or other device into *digital* signals that can be stored and processed by a home computer.

DISK A flat, circular object that resembles a phonograph record. A record "stores" music; a disk stores information. A disk is inserted into a *disk drive*, which rotates it at high speed. The drive *writes* new information onto the disk and *reads* information already stored on the disk. There are two major types of disks found on home computers: flexible *floppy disks*, and *hard disks*.

ERROR TRAPS Commands in your program that anticipate people making mistakes when they give answers to the computer. The commands test the people's answers to see if they're correct. If not, the commands print an *error message*, and the program loops back and asks for another answer.

EXECUTE Run. Process. Obey.

EXTERNAL MEMORY Also known as *mass memory* or *removable memory*. You use external memory to store programs and information that would otherwise be lost once your computer is turned off. Examples of external (non-RAM and non-ROM) memory include tape cassettes, disks, bubble, and CCD (charge-coupled) devices.

FILE A file is a collection of records all appearing under a single *file name*. All of the programs and data stored in external memory (on tape, disk, bubble, or CCD) are organized into files.

FLOPPY DISK (See *Disk*.)

FLOPPY DISK DRIVE (See *Disk*.)

FLOW CHART A diagram (of boxes and arrows) that shows the way your program is supposed to work.

GRAPHICS Pictures (as opposed to *text*—words and numbers).

HARDWARE The *machine* part of the computer: the wires, buttons, metal, blinking lights, etc. All of the computer *devices*.

INPUT DEVICE   Any machine that allows you to enter commands or information into the computer's main (RAM) memory. An input device could be a typewriter keyboard, an organ keyboard, a tape drive, a disk drive, a microphone, a light pen, a digitizer, or electronic *sensors*.

INTERFACE BOARD   A circuit board that allows you to hook the computer up to another machine, like a *modem* (to make phone calls), a typewriter, the house lights, or whatever. The interface board translates the signals from the two devices so that they can communicate with each other.

INTERPRETER   Like a compiler, an interpreter takes your (English-like) commands and translates them into machine-language instructions for the computer to process. Unlike a compiler, an interpreter (like *BASIC*) will process each command the moment it's entered.

LANGUAGE   Any unified, related set of commands that can be translated into machine-language instructions that the computer can process. There are lower-level languages that are difficult to use, but closely resemble the fundamental operations of a computer. There are higher-level languages that resemble English. There are *specialized languages* useful in performing particular tasks, *system languages* for controlling the operations of the computer, and *applications languages* that you use to write programs.

LED   Light Emitting Diode. LEDs are commonly used as control lights to indicate whether computer devices are off or on, active or inactive.

LOOP   A computer is in a loop when it obeys the same instructions in a program over and over. You can use a loop to print your name a thousand times, animate a figure on the picture screen, or repeat a game sequence. When a loop is under control, it is a powerful tool. Out of control, the loop may cause a program to loop forever (or, at least, until you enter an *interrupt* command, which frees the CPU from the loop). There can be loops inside of loops. These are called *nested loops*. The inside loop acts like a minute hand on a clock, while the outside loop acts like an hour hand.

LOOP COUNTER   A loop counter is a *variable*—a storage location, or address, in the computer's main (RAM) memory—that keeps track of how many times the program has processed the commands in the loop.

MACHINE LANGUAGE   A direct representation of electrical charges inside the computer. Machine language was the first computer language. It consists entirely of "1's" and "0's."

MAINFRAME   The box that houses the computer's main memory and logic components—its CPU, RAM, ROM, its interface and input-output (I/O) circuitry, and so on.

MILLISECOND   One thousandth of a second.

MODEL   A computer reproduction (or imitation) of a person, process, place, or thing in the real world, or in an imaginary world that you create. Models can be simple or complex; beautiful, educational, or just for fun; serious or part of a game. To model something: First learn about it, then describe it to the computer in the form of a program.

MODEM   MOdulator-DEModulator. A device that transforms a computer's electrical pulses into audible tones that are transmitted over a phone line to another computer. A modem also receives incoming tones and transforms them into electrical signals that can be processed and stored by the computer.

MONITOR   A *system* or *control* program that gives you several simple commands you can use to manage the computer. (See *Operating System*.)

MULTIPROCESSING   A home computer that has more than one CPU (Central Processing Unit) and is therefore able to obey several instructions simultaneously.

MULTIPROGRAMMING   A home computer that is able to run more than one program at a time. This allows more than one person to use the computer at a time, and it enables the computer to be engaged in more than one task at a time.

NATURAL LANGUAGE   A spoken language, like English, Spanish, Arabic, or Chinese. In the future it is likely that home computers will be fast enough and have big enough vocabularies to enable you to talk to them almost like you would talk to a person. There will no longer be a need for special *computer* languages.

NETWORK   A group of home computers communicating over telephone lines, or by use of radio or microwaves.

OPERATING SYSTEM   A *system* or *control* program that gives you a wide range of commands you can use to manage the computer and various input, output, and storage devices. You can use operating-system commands to copy, print, rename, and erase files; to create new files and edit old files; and to manage file space on external-memory devices, like tape and disk drives.

OUTPUT DEVICE   A machine that takes programs or information from the computer and transfers them to some other medium. Examples of output devices include tape, disk, and bubble-memory drives, computer printers, typewriters, and plotters, the computer picture screen (*video monitor*), robots (like the Terrapin *Turtle*), and sound-synthesis devices that enable the computer to talk and play music.

PASCAL   A high-level computer language (normally a compiler) developed by Niklaus Wirth and others in the early 1970s and named after the seventeenth-century French mathematician and philosopher, Blaise Pascal. *PASCAL* is a more *structured* and systematic language than *BASIC*, and is suitable for developing complicated model and game programs.

PIXEL   A "picture element." The computer picture screen is divided into rows and columns of tiny *dots*, *squares*, or *cells*. Each of these is a pixel.

PLOTTER   A computer device that uses a mechanical arm to draw pictures on paper. The plotter might use colored pens, jets of ink, heating coils, or even a laser beam.

PORT An outlet or *doorway* into (and out of) the computer. A connection point for electrical charges. A link between the computer and other devices.

PROGRAM A combination of one or more computer commands written in a particular computer language. A computer stores and processes a program as a unit.

RAM Random Access Memory. When you turn on the computer, the thousands of tiny storage cells in RAM are empty (filled with "o's"). Using program and operating-system commands, you can *load* programs and information into RAM, then relay them from RAM to the CPU, where they can be processed. When you turn off the computer, all of the programs and information in RAM are erased.

RECORD One or more pieces of related information stored in a computer file. Each file can contain one or more records. In a *program* file, each command in the program is a record. Records can be *read* from external memory (tape, disk, or bubble), one record at a time, and stored in RAM. Later (after processing) they can be *written* as part of a file back onto external memory.

RESOLUTION The number of pixels on the picture screen. A *high-resolution* picture looks smooth and realistic. It is produced by a large number of pixels (greater than sixty thousand). A *low-resolution* picture is blocky and jagged. It is produced by a small number of pixels.

ROM Read Only Memory. ROM chips are found in the computer's mainframe and inside *game packs* and *cartridges* that can be plugged into the computer. Any program or information stored in ROM is instantly available to the CPU for processing. Control programs (monitors and operating systems) are usually stored in ROM; your programming language (like *BASIC* or *PASCAL*) is probably stored in ROM; *canned* games and other programs are stored in ROM. ROM really is "read only." You can get programs and data from ROM, but you can't erase or change anything stored there.

SENSOR Any device that acts as "eyes" or "ears" for a home computer. Types of sensors include: *photoelectric sensors*, which are sensitive to light; *image sensor cameras*, which record visual images and transform the images into digital signals; *pressure sensors*, which are sensitive to any kind of pressure; *contact sensors*, which are sensitive to touch; *infrared sensors*, which record infrared radiation; and *ultrasonic transducers*, which produce a high-frequency sound wave that bounces off objects and lets the computer calculate the distance between itself and those objects.

SIMULATION A reproduction, image, or replica of something else. (See *Model*.)

SOFTWARE Computer programs.

SYNTHESIZER Any device that produces something based on digital signals stored in the computer. A *voice synthesizer* produces sounds that closely resemble a person talking. A *music synthesizer* makes music.

TAPE Magnetic, voice-grade (audio) tape found on tape cassettes. Used by many home computers as *external storage* for programs and data. Electrical signals from the computer are transformed into two tones (for a "1" and a "0"), then stored as magnetized segments on the tape. The segments can be reread later, converted into tones, then back into electrical signals that can be stored and processed by the computer.

TELETYPEWRITER TTY. Older computer typewriter. Used by many deaf people (without a computer connection) to make phone calls. TTYs are quickly being replaced by devices like the *C-Phone* (a small computer), which are faster and much more versatile.

VOICE RECOGNITION Any device that enables the computer to accept commands and information spoken over a microphone. (See *Synthesizer* and *Analog-to-Digital [A–D] Converter*.)

VOLTAGE Electrical pressure. High voltage in a computer circuit represents a "1"; low (or zero) voltage represents a "0."

A programmer/analyst and Ph.D. candidate in computer science, Fred D'Ignazio is part of a growing movement among computer professionals who want to see computers in the service of people in their homes.

As the father of two young children, he has become concerned with introducing the computer to young people as a wonderful tool rather than as a forbidding electronic device. He lives with his wife and family in Chapel Hill, North Carolina.

INDEX